KISS THE WAVE
by Tara Leigh Cobble

Published by Shrinking Music Publishing
A Division of Shrinking Music
taraleighcobble.com
© copyright 2014
Design by Marlena Sigman at MarlenaSigman.com
Layout by Lore Ferguson at Sayable.net
Author Photo by Jeremy Cowart at JeremyCowart.com
ALL RIGHTS RESERVED
No part of this publication may be reproduced, stored in a retrieval system, or transmitted, in any form or by any means – electronic, mechanical, photocopying, recording, or otherwise – without prior written permission.
International Standard Book Number: 978-1-4951-3339-8
Printed in the United States of America

THIS BOOK IS DEDICATED TO D-GROUP.
PURSUING THE LORD ALONGSIDE YOU
IS ONE OF MY GREATEST JOYS.

CONTENTS

INTRODUCTION	11
1. ROCK	15
2. GOD OF SECRETS	21
3. EXCEEDING JOY	27
4. FORGIVER	31
5. STEADFAST LOVE	37
6. FATHER	41
7. SLOW TO ANGER	47
8. GRACIOUS	51
9. BLESSED HOPE	55
10. SAVIOR	59
11. MERCIFUL	65
12. MASTER	69
13. PORTION	73
14. LORD OF HOSTS	79
15. SOURCE	83
16. GOOD SHEPHERD	87
17. WONDERFUL COUNSELOR	99
18. RESTORER	105
19. PROVIDER	113
20. HEALER	117
21. HUSBAND	127
22. LIGHT	133
23. FRIEND	137
24. SONG	141
25. HOLY	145
26. RIGHTEOUSNESS	149
27. STRENGTH	155
28. SOVEREIGN	159

29.	KIND	167
30.	MAN OF SORROWS	171
31.	STABILITY	175
32.	PEACE	183
33.	LIFE	187
34.	GUIDE	191
35.	GIVER	197
36.	KEEPER	199
37.	FREEDOM	205
38.	THE GOD WHO SEES	211
39.	REWARDER	217
40.	REWARD	223

ACKNOWLEDGEMENTS

BOOK CONTRIBUTORS:

Steven Naimark, Becky Wilson, Raicheal Sutherland – who scoured these pages for grammatical and theological inaccuracies. Marlena Sigman, Jeremy Cowart – for your gifts at design. Lore Ferguson – for all of the above, plus steak.

THOSE WHO MADE SPAIN HOME FOR ME WHILE I WROTE THIS BOOK:

Michelle and Brian King, Amanda Hannah, Josiah Walcott, Aretta Zitta, Diane Michaelis, Laura Reisinger, Storey Thompson, Abby Mayfield, Lt. Chaplain Tim Miller, Brindo mi Vida, NavSta Rota, PWOC Rota, MCYM / Club Beyond Europe

THIS BOOK WOULD NOT HAVE BEEN POSSIBLE WITHOUT:

The Village Church, Matt Chandler, D-Groups, Kemper Crabb, Judy Scheuch, RLDG (which does not exist), Roots Coffee HV, Jay and Melanie McWhorter, Mike West, Lee McDerment, Chrissy and J.D. Smith, Caroline Coleman, Alex Brandt, Sam Harrison

MY PRAYER TEAM:

Lauren Chandler, Candice Romo, Cherie Duffey, Patsy Glunt, Meghann Glenn, Lauren Schroeder, Maggie Shaffer, Becca Bailey, Hannah Elmore, Lexi Bassinger

MY DEEPEST GRATITUDE TO:

- The Lord: my constant, my treasure.

- My family: who graciously let me write about some of the deepest sorrows we've stumbled through together. I love you all, and it's my joy to share your name.

- Those who appear on these pages: for being the means through which God reveals so much of Himself to me. You've enhanced my love for Him by your presence.

> *"I HAVE LEARNED TO KISS THE WAVE THAT STRIKES ME AGAINST THE ROCK OF AGES."*
>
> CHARLES SPURGEON

INTRODUCTION

What was the moment when everything in your life divided into a story of before and after?

Was it when the beautiful thing you longed for finally came into your grasp? Or was it an emotional shipwreck, the waves throwing your storm-drunk heart against the rocks as you gasped for breath?

Achieved goals can be life-shaping, but trials have the potential to be all the more spiritually formative. They reveal to us whether we suffer well or not, whether we reach for God in the darkness or if we've trusted too much in a ship filled with holes. Often, it's only in the aftermath – when the clouds have cleared away and we're nursing our wounds – that we have the presence of mind to notice where we've landed.

If we lean into bitterness and entitlement when the waves bury us, we become more embittered, more entitled. Years pass, and we petrify. But if we lean into humility and forgiveness and trust, we soften. Time multiplies and colonizes whatever we've been growing in our hearts.

Not only are trials and joys what shape our hearts, but they are also what reveal our hearts to us. If you tip a glass over, the only thing that can spill out of it is what it contains. In the same way, when our lives get tipped over, what's inside pours out for everyone to see. Our responses to life's trials reveal who we believe God to be.

If I never look to God when I'm fearful, then it doesn't really matter that Christ is the Prince of Peace. If I only want to pursue my own desires instead of yielding to God, then I never get to experience the joy of having the Spirit as my Guide. If I live mindful of Him, though, I will see Him being who He says He is.

Each time His actions testify to His character, I aim to carry the experience forward and remind myself that He lived up to His names. In ancient times, names represented character. Our God is not misnamed – He really is all the things Scripture says of Him. Each of the 40 chapters in this book extols a different name of God or an aspect of His character, as they were revealed to me through normal life events.

I hope these stories will encourage you; but more than I want you to see where God showed up in my life, I want you to learn to look for Him in your own. If we are attentive, I believe we will see, multiplied over time, how far God Himself has carried us. We will learn more about His character and His personality, making every joy or tragedy an opportunity for greater depth in our relationship with Him.

That belief is what prompts me to use part of Charles Spurgeon's quote as the title of this book. I will embrace these moments, knowing they reveal more of God to me and attach my heart more fully to Him.

I wrote the Reflection Questions at the end of each chapter to help you identify times when God has been your Exceeding Joy or your Healer or your Strength. If you haven't seen Him be those things yet, I hope the questions will give you a lens to look for His character when He displays it in the future. You can ponder the reflection questions on your own, but I think they serve a greater purpose when you discuss them with a group of other Christ-followers. Press into the hard questions. Ask God to reveal Himself to you and to be these things for you.

My prayer for all of us is that we may be students of Him and His great pursuit of us. May He give us eyes to see The Gospel of Christ worked out not just in our salvation, but in the subtle moments of each numbered day. Look for Him everywhere.

1
ROCK

Trust in The LORD forever,
for The LORD GOD is an everlasting rock.
Isaiah 26:4

Few things have the power to highlight your flaws quite like living with Swedish nobility.

I moved into Swedish Lisa's two-bedroom bungalow in South Carolina during her last six months in the States, and it was the closest I'll ever get to rooming with Princess Kate or Sophia Loren. Lisa was well-traveled and sophisticated and astute. Even though English was her third language, she was more articulate than me on most days.

Her decorating style was the stuff of *Modern Architecture*. That was likely due to her noble lineage, combined with whatever IKEA pumped into the Scandinavian water supply when she was a child.

Nothing hung on a wall or sat on a shelf without serving a function. The living room was wall-to-wall white, yet somehow it still felt inviting and liveable. Every candle and rug and piece of art in was intentionally chosen to contribute to the stark-meets-luxurious aesthetic – clean lines with intermittent pops of neutrals or vibrant color.

I tried to adopt her style as my own. When people walked into my bedroom, they often said things like, "You need a vase on that table," or "Are you going to hang a picture there?" while pointing to the empty wall above my headboard. I never heeded their advice, and Lisa and I were both happier for it.

One day I bought a sleek pewter clock for my bedroom wall. When I got home, I rummaged through the toolbox to find a hammer and nail, then pulled a step stool from the laundry room. I tucked the clock safely under my chin (it was approximately 14" in diameter – larger than a dinner plate), and stepped onto the stool. I stood on my tiptoes – head down, for fear the clock would fall from underneath my chin, arms fully stretched upward – to nail the clock above my door frame.

I heard the front door open, and Lisa let out a sing-song "Hel-loooooooo," as she arrived home from work.

"I'm in my room," I half-yelled, trying not to drop the clock. When she appeared in my open doorway, I had just finished nailing the hole in the wall.

"What are you doing?" she said, laughing at my bodily contortions.

"I'm hanging my new clock!" I said, satisfied. I pulled the clock from underneath my chin and hung it on the nail.

Lisa stepped through the doorway and turned to look at the clock. "So, um … did you measure that first?" she asked, trying to suppress a chuckle.

"No, why?"

"Come down from the stool and see."

It was at least six inches left of center, and four inches too high. "Uh … oops?" I said.

She rested her hand on my shoulder and said, "Well, there's one thing about you – at least you get the job done."

"In this instance, I'm not sure if that's a pro or a con." I said, laughing along with her.

"Let's just say you do things, um … fast and wrong."

"Fast and wrong," I said, nodding. "Yes. That is a fairly succinct summary of all my strengths and weaknesses." I tilted my head and wrinkled my nose as I looked at the clock again. "That placement definitely will annoy me. Can you help me fix it?"

She pulled her hair back into a ponytail, brought in her laser level and measuring tape and a small tub of sheetrock filler, and spent the next half hour undoing the damage it took me two minutes to do.

To this day, I notice "fast and wrong" creeping up in many of my natural tendencies. I've always hated the thought of being lazy or passive, so my innate response when I see a problem or a task is to take action. However, if I don't take time to weigh the consequences or analyze my options more closely, I'm bound to end up far from the ideal and filled with regret.

—

In Matthew 7:24-27, Jesus's disciples have gathered around Him, and He's giving them a talk we call The Sermon on the Mount. At the very end of His three-chapter monologue describing what it looks like to follow Him, Jesus gives the disciples two options: build your life around things that fall apart, or build your life around things that last. He says the first option is like building your house on sand, and the second option is like building your house on a rock. The disciples had access to the Old Testament Scriptures, which repeatedly referred to God as the Rock, so Jesus was presenting a fairly straight forward analogy.

Even the apostles, who spent most of their free time with Jesus, still faced the temptation to build their lives on something altogether different — something not powerful enough to heal the blind and raise the dead. Their desires beckoned them to pursue lesser, weaker joys. One of them gave in to the love of money, another gave in to protect himself and his reputation. If we look closely enough at what they tried to build their lives around in those instances, we find that it was, at its root, themselves.

I'm a pretty lousy thing to build my life around. I let myself down, choose poorly, and don't follow through. Most of my desires are oriented around fleeting pleasures, proving that my current desires may bring me no thrill when tomorrow arrives. My life, if built on me, is built on sand.

The deceptive thing about sand is that it appears to be rock at first glance. It's so densely compressed that it easily fools the untrained eye. Only when the storm comes does the sand reveal its secret: *I am not stable. I am going to shift and crumble and rip apart everything that dares to rest on me.*

When pastors teach on this passage from Scripture, they often mention that the storm comes for everyone eventually — even those on the Rock. There's another shared experience in this parable, though: both people have to invest time and energy and resources and hope into building something.

To build on rock you have to dig down deep. It is a labor of patience, sustained by the desire for something lasting. It is anything but "fast and wrong." Digging into rock may be exhausting, but it will never be as heartbreaking as watching everything you love slide into the ocean.

———

I've had many a landslide in my short life, because I'm especially gifted in the idolatry department, and God is too generous not to deal with me on that. Repeatedly, I've tried to anchor down in some dream or role or relationship. Sometimes God brought a gentle rain to erode my false hopes; but sometimes, if I resisted His conviction for long enough, He brought a tidal wave to dissolve all my sandcastles. Sometimes I even washed out to sea along with them.

Then, because He isn't content to have His children floating aimlessly, He sends another wave to throw me back to the Rock. *"There's a home for you here,"* is what He seems to whisper. *"Dig deep into this instead. Stay."*

The greatest thing I've ever done was to begin digging in the Rock. I want to weary myself with learning Him. He is worth every effort to know Him more, because unlike all my lesser loves, the storms do not erode Him – they reveal Him.

Everything else is fast and wrong; but He is eternal and steady and perfect.

For who is God, but The Lord? And who is a rock, except our God?
- Psalm 18:31

REFLECTION QUESTIONS:

1. What "houses" have you built on the sand? In retrospect, what was the result of that?

2. How did that impact your relationship with God? Did you ever feel angry that God wasn't content to let you live in that spot forever?

3. What hopes and dreams do you have that may someday disappoint you, even if they are fulfilled?

4. What has God revealed to you about Himself through the storms you've endured?

2
GOD OF SECRETS

The friendship (or secret counsel) of the Lord is for those who fear Him.
Psalm 25:14

Have you ever felt like God was telling you a secret?

—

I pulled at the hotel's white quilted down comforter, reeling in the remote control, while trying not to overturn the half empty box of General Tso's chicken just beyond my reach. "The Colbert Report" was wrapping up, and I needed the mute button.

The Venetian in Las Vegas was the nicest hotel I'd ever stayed in. For three days, I never left the hotel grounds. The promoter of a concert booked my room there, but when I finally arrived in the middle of the night, after a 15-hour drive, the hotel had already given my room away. To compensate for the inconvenience, they put me up in the Penthouse Suite. *The Penthouse Suite.*

After I managed to avoid spilling my Chinese takeout on the mattress that cost more than I make in a year, I muted the 32" flatscreen, and grabbed my Bible and red journal from the Victorian oak table at my bedside.

In the months prior, God had been healing me from a long heartache and the fears that cropped up in the aftermath. Being away from home, alone on tour, provided a bittersweet kind of therapy – I had more time alone with God to talk to Him, listen to sermons on the drive, read my Bible uninterrupted. Still, I ached for the kind of familiarity only home could bring. I longed for the slow evenings where a small group of friends gathered around a dinner table, sharing the bread and the wine and the solid foundation that held us up despite our common struggles.

God faithfully carried me through months of touring during that season of loss, letting me feel lonely but never alone. His Word spoke to me clearly sometimes, and at other times I felt His prompting in dreams, via songs, or even through the Holy Spirit speaking to me in my thoughts.

When I sense God may be speaking, His words come to me with heavy footsteps, but I take care not to let my impressions of His words fall heavier on my heart than Scripture. Scripture is His certain word, and my impressions must be weighed against it – never contradicting it, only reinforcing the truths I have already seen it reveal. Anything I perceive as being from Him must bear the test of time: if it proves true, it was Him, and if it doesn't, it was me.

I describe His voice as a "bold-font voice," which is how I distinguish it from my own. As I've gotten to know Him better, I've found that His bold-font voice frequently affirms and reiterates the things He says in Scripture – encouragement, guidance, conviction – and often uses the same words. This is one of the many ways memorizing and meditating on Scripture serves us well, because then God is re-speaking a language we already know.

In my Las Vegas hotel room that day, the first thing I felt Him say was: *This is very important. Write down everything I say.*

I pulled out my journal and wrote: "This is very important. Write down everything I say." Then I waited, my pen poised for the next words He might speak.

Saczang.

I wrote it down, wondering, *"Hmm... saczang? What does that word mean? It must be a word I don't know yet."* So I grabbed my laptop, opened a dictionary website, and searched the word. *"Nope. That's not a word, God."*

I leaned forward, stuffed another pillow behind my back to sit upright, and drummed my fingers on the keyboard, perplexed.

"Maybe this is a foreign language?" I wondered. *"He knows all the languages, right?"*

I went to a translation site and selected "detect language." It came up empty.

As a final effort, I did an internet search on the word. Google yielded only one result. I stared at the lone blue link followed by an empty page of white and clicked the link.

It took me to the Chamber of Commerce website for a small town in Poland called Nowy Sacz. On the site, there was a PDF explaining some upcoming changes in the town. The site also had an English (or as they call it, Angielski) translation of the document, which was very helpful since I couldn't read Polish. The English document was titled "SaczAng" ("Sacz" for the name of the town and "Ang" for the English/Angielski translation). According to Google, that site was the only place on the internet where that particular combination of letters occurred.

It felt like God had given me a decoder ring for this unusual message. Intrigued, I set the Chinese takeout boxes on the table, turned off the muted television, and rolled over onto my stomach, my laptop at my left hand, my Bible and journal at my right hand. I inhaled, prayed.

I clicked to open the PDF. "There will now be a new Nowy Sacz." The town was about to undergo a complete renovation in every area aimed at "restoring its former beauty and magnificence." I wrote the entire text of the PDF in my journal, set my pen down and read over the words several times.

"Why are You telling me this? I've never even been to Poland. What do You want me to learn about You in this?"

It was one of the most unusual, perplexing things I'd ever felt like God had spoken to me. I didn't tell anyone for over a year. I hid it in my heart as I watched and waited.

—

For those who know God, "fear of The Lord" is comprised primarily of delight and awe. When we see the magnitude of our Father and the beauty of His affection toward us, we're drawn in. He beckons us to come closer so He can whisper into our hearts.

David exhibited this delight and awe when he wrote about the fear of The Lord in Psalm 86.

For You are great and do wondrous things; You alone are God. Teach me Your way, O Lord, that I may walk in Your truth; unite my heart to fear Your name. I give thanks to You, O Lord my God, with my whole heart, and I will glorify Your name forever. - Psalm 86:10-12.

At the time, I didn't know what "saczang" would really entail. I waited for Him to reveal how the secret would play out. What followed was a complete uprooting of everything in my life, the overturning of everything I thought I knew and understood – desires, relationships, my identity*. Had He not whispered that secret in my ear or given me the grace to pay attention to it, I don't know how I would've survived the months that came afterward.

In speaking that one word to me, God pulled back the curtain to

**I tell the detailed story of this "uprooting" in my memoir,* Orange Jumpsuit: Letters to the God of Freedom.

show me a bit of what He was doing in my life. All the renovations, all the uprooting – it was aimed at restoring my former beauty and magnificence. That is to say: the image of God in me.

God cares about His kids. Really cares. He is gentle with our hearts. He speaks. If we listen, we'll hear Him. In John 10:27, Jesus talks about this very thing. He says, *"My sheep hear my voice, and I know them, and they follow Me."* I feel it – I feel known by Him. I'm grateful that the God of Secrets whispered one in my ear, like a close friend and confidant. His words help me see how attentive He is to the heart He knows so well.

REFLECTION QUESTIONS:

1. Have you ever felt like God was speaking to you directly?

2. What wisdom do you seek to discern the voice of God? How do you know if you've heard the Spirit's prompting or something else?

3. Have you ever been wrong about something you thought you heard God say?

4. What does "the fear of The Lord" look like to you?

3
EXCEEDING JOY

Then I will go to the altar of God, to God, my exceeding joy.
Psalm 43:4

"Find the things that stir your affections for Christ and saturate your life in them. Find the things that rob you of that affection and walk away from them. That's the Christian life as easy as I can explain it for you."
Matt Chandler

A stranger from the internet picked me up at the Orlando airport around midnight.

The plan had only come together in the previous 48 hours. Karen, an effervescent woman with white-blonde hair and two grown daughters, had read one of my books and friended me on Facebook. She noticed my affinity for NASA and space travel, and she decided, with the support of her husband, to send me an email the week before NASA closed down its shuttle program:

"Since you talk about NASA all the time on Facebook, I'm just throwing this out there for your consideration because God has not left me alone about it! We live directly across from the shuttle launch pad at Kennedy Space Center, and would like to invite you to come watch STS-135, the final shuttle launch, with us – I'll handle all the arrangements and accommodations. I'm not in the habit of making this kind of offer. As a matter of fact this is the first time. We would love to have you, for as long as you'd like to stay."

I almost turned it down, but not for the reasons most people would think. I wasn't wary of being in the home of a stranger so much as I was concerned about commonplace launch delays due to weather or mechanical difficulties. I didn't want to fly to Florida to see the final launch, only to have it delayed.

The launch forecast said there was a 30% chance of delay or rescheduling, but I prayed hard, printed my ticket, and boarded my flight to meet Karen and her daughter in Orlando later that night. They picked me up, and we began the drive to Titusville, while I tried to suppress my excitement.

The drive took longer than it should've, mostly because of the crowds – RVs lined the streets, people camped alongside the road, tents punctuated the grassy medians, teams of people tossed frisbees and footballs across the highway. As we snail-paced our way down the four-lane, I peered out the windows. I slid left and right on the empty backseat, alternating driver's side and passenger's side views, just to drink it all in. I realized I'd been holding my eyes wide, as though I wanted to maximize even my peripheral views.

"I love that you get to experience this," Karen said. "You just have so much *wonder*. That's how we feel too, even though we've lived here and seen this for years. It never gets old."

"Are you bummed that it's ending?" I asked.

"We can hardly believe it. The entire town economy will shift." She paused. "It's the end of an era."

I could feel her sadness, so I stopped sliding across the backseat.

"The good news," she continued, "is that my friend Michelle, who has an even better view from her condo, is going to let us watch from her balcony! She said you can spend the night there, too."

Two hours later, we stood in Michelle's kitchen sharing life stories. She offered me herbal tea, but I requested black coffee instead. I didn't want to sleep. Over Karen's shoulder, I saw the lights through the balcony's sliding glass doors – the orange and white glow of the shuttle, lit from below, majestic and poised for liftoff.

I retired to the guest bedroom with what remained of my coffee, but long after everyone fell asleep, I climbed out of bed and snuck into the living room. Every hour or so, I'd get up to look at it again. I took so many pictures that I depleted my phone battery, which served as a testament to the sheer delight outweighing my logic. A shuttle on a launch pad doesn't change positions, so all of my 120 pictures were only slight variations of each other.

I tried to let each of my senses engage so I could fully feel the moment. The humid Florida night air, the salty smell of the Atlantic on the wind, the excited din of the people camping 12 stories below the balcony. We were all thinking the same thing ... *Launch*.

One of my favorite occurrences is when everyone you encounter is thinking the same thing. It's rare. It doesn't happen at sporting events, because there are opposing teams. It doesn't happen in politics or entertainment. It barely even happens at weddings. But occasionally you have a moment where everyone is on the same page, and it feels like a little glimpse into the Kingdom, where all our hearts will reverberate with one thought: *HIM*.

—

Four hours later, after a cloud-stained sunrise, Michelle led me out through the floods of people to buy a commemorative t-shirt, then we walked across the bridge, which was closed to traffic and stacked with people. I was giddy with anticipation. I high-fived strangers. The crowd below buzzed at full volume. When we made it back to her condo, Karen was already there with the balcony open and the TV tuned to the NASA network. We kept one eye on the TV broadcast and one eye on the launch pad. No sign of a delay yet. I kept praying.

The countdown clock could be stopped at any second, and tragedy could strike at any moment afterward. Such a delicate procedure. Yet there we stood, hopeful –

"10 … 9 … 8 … 7… 6 … 5 …" The engines fired.

"4 … 3 … 2 … 1 … 0 … And liftoff!" the television announced.

Shouts of joy from the ground below, the balconies above, all around. I breathed deep, relieved, as tears came to my eyes. The beauty of those moments isn't just in the experience itself; it's also in the sweetness of a God who engineered the circumstances. He had given me a front row seat for NASA's final shuttle launch by prompting a stranger from the internet to reach out to me. How generous of Him, knowing my heart like He does, to give me an opportunity I'd always wanted but never even thought to ask Him for.

He built the things space shuttles venture to see. He created the minds that invented space shuttles. The whole event was an unveiling of God's brilliance – all the glory and all the exceeding joy pointed back to Him. Maybe everyone there didn't know that, but I did. And I rejoiced.

I will greatly rejoice in the LORD; my soul shall exult in my God. - Isaiah 61:10

REFLECTION QUESTIONS:

1. What are some things that stir your affection for The Lord?

2. In what ways has God shown you He is attentive to your heart?

3. What big prayers have you been afraid to pray? Why? What might be the benefit of asking Him for those things?

4
FORGIVER

*Be kind to one another, tenderhearted,
forgiving one another, as God in Christ forgave you.*
Ephesians 4:32

John Piper, a white-haired, wiry-framed pastor that I podcast, likes to emphasize his points by alternating a whisper and a booming voice. It makes it difficult to listen to him on headphones without ripping them off every five minutes, but it's worth it.

Once, in his gentle whispery voice, he said something about forgiveness that stuck with me. He said a lot of people hesitate to forgive because they misunderstand what forgiveness is. He said people think it means they have to act like what happened was okay, when in most cases, the thing that we're forgiving is actually a sin; and by God's standards, those are never "okay." He said it's fitting and right to be angry about what happened – about the sin – but the act of forgiveness is choosing to release the desire to punish that other person for their sin, and leaving the outcome in God's hands.

Unforgiveness, on the other hand, is a feeling of superiority that says, "I would never do that terrible thing you did. I am better than you." Humility and unforgiveness can't grow in the same heart – one will eventually overtake the other.

I played that part of the podcast over a few times, to let it sink in. I knew I had to contend with the lie of superiority in my heart, because it had begun to take root.

Joel was the last man I dated, and the last man I thought I might ever date, but things began to fall apart even as they were only beginning. The short story is he said he wasn't ready; the long story is I wasn't ready to believe him.

I've never lost anything so slowly. It was more like a terminal illness than a heart attack. By the time he was finally gone, he was still as real and tangible as ever. There was a frustrating lack of difference between the memory and the reality, the shadow and the form. I couldn't be sure – especially since I hadn't seen him or spoken to him in more than six months – but I thought I still cared for him.

In the same breath, though, there was anger, thick and dense. It might've been hatred. I've only ever hated two people, and both of them were people I once loved. "Hate" doesn't work between members of God's Family, I know. We are called to hate only the things God hates, and He certainly loves His kids, so I can't love Him while also nurturing hatred toward any of His family. At the same time, I also knew I couldn't lie to Him, because He knew how I felt, so I decided to be honest with Him and ask Him to help me change. I would rather talk to Him about it than try to fake it, because there's no hope in dishonesty, and because He's the only person who can make my heart work right anyway. He hears my honest prayers, and edits my heart in the process.

I journaled about it:

Why can't I forgive Joel? Why am I so cynical about it?

I looked at the questions. I drew a line under them and asked God to help me.

I am the single greatest cause of my own cynicism. The reason I think people don't deserve forgiveness is because I know I haven't deserved it. I don't trust others or their motives because I see what is inside of myself, and I know how well I can fool other people.

It's easy to find scapegoats and pin my cynicism on others. I tie it to the heads of people in my past who have hurt me, because some never apologized or owned what they did. But I know it's my own reluctance to forgive people that solidifies my cynicism.

I could try to pin the blame on Joel, even though he had been honest with me from the start, but the person I study most closely, and spend all my time with, and get most of my evidence from is myself. If I can't even get my heart to obey God in forgiving Joel, why would I expect Joel to be able to change his own heart? I am not superior to him. I am just as broken.

Didn't we all think we'd be different by now? Weren't we feeding ourselves daydreams of our ideal selves and lives? Yet we wake to the same old shadows, the same regrets and mistakes, the same pain.

Every stalled out attempt at healing and wholeness only serves to cement my cynicism. Another failure. I can only throw myself onto the bloodied back of Christ. He will carry me – cynicism and failures and wounds – until all is redeemed. And throughout the carrying, He transforms my heart.

John 15 says He has the greatest love of all: He laid down His life. The least I can do is lay down my grudge.

God, help me obey You. Help me forgive him like You have forgiven me.

As much as I ached from my relationship with Joel, much of that was the result of my own decisions and brokenness.

Years ago, my therapist told me something else about forgiveness that I've never forgotten. "Forgiveness is a decision to embark on a journey," he said. "It isn't arrival, it isn't completion. It is the journey, a thousand times over."

I wondered: would forgiving Joel mean seeking his friendship again? I didn't feel ready for that. Would forgiving him mean telling him I'd forgiven him? Or was that supposed to be between me and God?

I decided to write him a letter, telling him I'd forgiven him. Instead, what came out was an apology. The forgiveness God told me to offer him led to the realization of so many sins I had committed in our relationship – some of which were sins between me and God, but which affected the way I'd treated Joel.

Joel,

The ways I've sinned against you have been many, and I'm truly broken over it. It took me a while to get past the bitterness, to find that I've been arrogant and entitled in my thoughts toward you. I'm overwhelmed at the depth of my sinfulness, and I'm sorry for the way those sinful thoughts have prompted my divisive attitude.

I don't expect you to trust my motives in this, and I can't expect you to forgive me. That's okay. I don't need anything from you, not even a reply. I trust that His work in me – to break me over my sins and to ask for forgiveness from the one I have offended – is the reason I'm supposed to write this letter.

- TLC

I felt God's forgiveness, which informs and enables my own, even toward myself. To not forgive myself would mean I had a higher standard of behavior than a holy God, which is both prideful and impossible. I knew I would be okay if Joel didn't forgive me, but I couldn't imagine that he wouldn't at least try. Because more than we are people who have hurt each other, we are part of God's family. There is unity even today, which will be fully realized in the Kingdom, even if we can't find the grace to acknowledge it now.

He has delivered us from the domain of darkness and transferred us to the Kingdom of His beloved Son, in whom we have redemption, the forgiveness of sins. - Colossians 1:13-14

REFLECTION QUESTIONS:

1. Are there people you need to forgive? What does it look like for you to walk that out?

2. Are there people you need to apologize to and ask forgiveness from? What does it look like for you to walk that out?

3. How does the Father's forgiveness of you (through the relationship He established with you in Christ) inform the way you view your sins and regrets? Is it hard to get your emotions to line up with the truth? Why or why not?

5
STEADFAST LOVE

The steadfast love of The Lord never ceases;
His mercies never come to an end;
they are new every morning;
great is Your faithfulness.
Lamentations 3:22-23

Steadfast love is certain love. It's unchanging. Not temperamental. It doesn't fluctuate based on my attitude or actions. It can be depended on from day to day. I will not wake tomorrow to a sudden change in God's feelings or commitment toward me. I will wake to the same mercy, the same love, the same faithfulness, renewed over again from an endless supply.

Nothing else in my life is like this. Absolutely nothing. Not the weather, not the economy, not any of my earthly relationships. Nothing is a guarantee except Him. Everything else has been outed as a lousy god, because worshipping something undependable can only leave me fearful, despairing. What a waste of worship.

I wonder what it felt like to be the God of all certainty, walking among those who don't possess the kind of information He did. I journaled about it:

Jesus, did You know uncertainty? Because that's the thing I have the hardest time with down here. Your Word says when You walked in gravity, You were tempted in every way we are. Can an omniscient God-Man know what it's like to feel curious and hopeful? Maybe that doesn't count as temptation?

Or did You suspend omniscience while You were on earth? And if so, was it selective suspension? Because You knew the thoughts and motives and life stories of strangers. You saw Nathanael under the fig tree. You responded in conversation to people's unspoken thoughts. You knew who touched Your robe, and You knew what you would endure on the cross. You knew things only God knows, because You Are.

But You still had to learn things like how to lace Your sandals or how to bait a hook, right? What about Scripture? Did You know that all already or did You struggle to memorize it like we do?

You know the world as certainties, fixed in place by the Father. I know the world as questions, waiting to see what He has sovereignly determined. If You had everything mapped out while You were on earth, I feel a little bit less understood. Help me. I want to feel known too. And I want to know You more than everything.

One of the great things about God's omniscience is that I can't shock Him. Nothing catches Him off guard. Humans aren't like that. We have to wait to see how things will unfold.

As I held my apology letter to Joel in my left hand, I rifled through my desk drawer with my right hand, looking for an envelope. The only special envelopes I have are small, pale pink squares. Those seemed too personal. But the alternative was a legal-size business envelope. Too sterile and stoic. I didn't want to get in the way of how Joel perceived the letter. I wanted it to speak for itself. Maybe I was over-analyzing.

I decided to err on the side of softness. I folded the letter and put it into the pale pink envelope, then tucked it into the pocket of my purse, along with a few apologies I had written to other people. There was no way to know when I might see him again, but I wanted to hand-deliver it.

A few weeks passed, then one night at church, I saw him leaving, only a few feet ahead of me.

"Joel," I called out past the people between us.

He turned and stopped, surprised to see me looking at him. The dense crowd pushed past him like a river, while he stood unmoved, a stone. I flowed with the crowd of people until I caught up to him.

"This is for you," I said, holding out the letter.

"Thanks," he said. Or maybe I just imagined it.

I had no idea how he would respond, if at all, or even what he might think.

It's safe to be undone by something trustworthy and reliable like God's steadfast love. Though the world may not call it safe (because it doesn't guarantee a painless outcome, which is how the world views safety), but it's eternally safe. By which I mean: no matter the outcome of giving Joel the letter – whether he accepted my offering or not – I knew I was held by the steadfast love of The Lord.

God loved me steadfastly through every moment of my sin toward Joel, every time I leaned into the bitterness. God loved Joel steadfastly too. We are both His kids, and we both get new mercies every day, drawn from the same fountain.

That night, I lay in bed and journaled:

"But all I ever learned from love
was how to shoot somebody who outdrew you."
- Leonard Cohen, "Hallelujah"

I'm unlearning all I learned, all I spent my life rehearsing. I'm carried on the back of the Forgiveness that forgave me. I'm praying blessing, asking for bounty and joy for all those who have hurt me. I'm begging for healing and hope for those I've hurt. I'm praying His steadfast love meets us in the darkest corners of our hearts and pours His light out.

May He undo all I've done, heal all I've broken, bless all I've cursed.

Leonard Cohen called it "a cold and broken hallelujah." But it's a hallelujah nonetheless. And all the more.

I slid my journal onto the shelf of my bedside table, switched the lamp off, and pulled the covers over my head. Just as I was falling asleep, I heard my phone beep. It was an instant message.

Tara-Leigh, I just want to say thank you for the letter you gave me. I appreciate your vulnerability and humility. I could write you and confess many ways I've wronged you as well, but my heart's desire isn't to find or expose faults in either of us. Regardless, thank you. I really do appreciate your words.

I slid my phone back onto the night stand and rolled onto my side, a few tears of relief pooled in the spot where my eye rested against the pillow.

Hallelujah.

REFLECTION QUESTIONS:

1. Has there been a time when you've doubted God's steadfast love for you? Was it because of something you did, something He did, or something else?

2. What Scriptures encourage you and speak the truth to you when you think you are under His wrath?

3. Since God knows everything, including the future, is it ever possible for you to disappoint Him?

6
FATHER

You have received the Spirit of adoption as sons,
by whom we cry, "Abba! Father!"
The Spirit Himself bears witness with our spirit
that we are children of God.
Romans 8:15b-16

I arrived at church early one Sunday to serve with the worship team. I watched as the audio visual team rolled through the video of the day's announcements to make sure it worked properly. In the first segment, there was an announcement that sent my heart racing: my pastor was taking a group to Israel, and there were 200 spots open.

I ran to the back of the auditorium and slid into the quiet of the foyer as I dialed my parents' phone number. My dad led trips to Israel for more than two decades, and he had always wanted me to go. He promised me a trip there when I was in college, but with classes all week and touring on the weekends, the timing never worked out.

My words came out like a flood. "Poppy! I know it's early so I hope I didn't wake you, but my church is taking a trip to Israel and I want to go. Do you think I should go? You're the expert on these things, so I wanted to ask you first. Should I go? I really think I should go. Can I cash in my college trip? Can I? Can I?" I was five years old again.

He wanted to know details. How much was the trip? Did it include airfare? How many days? What sites would we be seeing?

In my excitement, I had completely failed to notice all the important information. I started grabbing volunteers and janitors, asking around. "Did you see that Israel video? How much was it? When was it?"

I stood bouncing from foot to foot at the guest services desk in the church lobby while I finished talking through the details of the trip with dad. I logged onto the computer and signed up for the trip only ten minutes after they gave the announcement reel its test run.

—

Tel Aviv smelled like orange groves. The air was the same temperature as the surface of my skin – perfect, light. We rolled our bags to the bus and fought the jet lag with several rounds of Israeli coffee, two ounces of thick espresso at a time.

As we walked from the bus to our hotel, we laughed, removed our sunglasses, widened our eyes. We sighed, exhaling delight and awe. I was taken aback by the way it felt to be there. The atmosphere juxtaposed weightlessness and gravity.

Most of my travel revolved around my singing and speaking schedule, so I wondered if I was simply caught up in the vacation-like feel of it all. But that didn't explain how a country that was objectively dangerous felt like a cocoon of peace and ease? I couldn't comprehend it. None of us could. We marveled.

As the days passed, we paused in wonder at many of the sites where Jesus lived and walked and taught. One day we stood underneath the shade of a tree in the Garden of Gethsemane as our tour guide told us the tree was more than 2,000 years old. It was there when Jesus prayed in the Garden on the night before His crucifixion. It was there for the tears, for the prayers of agony while His friends were sleeping, for the kiss of betrayal.

Being where He once was opened something inside of me – hints of passion and deep longing. That, too, caught me off guard, but this time I knew where to pin it. It reminded me of something I'd felt before, though it was much stronger this time.

When I was in college, my heart was knit to the guy who had slowly become my best friend. He fell for me too, but we kept our secrets separately. I, out of desire for him to pursue me. He, because he knew he would be flying around the whole big world to spend the summer as a missionary in Papua New Guinea, and he didn't want to tie up our summer with distraction.

He told me his secret over the Chinese dinner we cooked together on his first day back for the fall semester. I didn't tell him then, but I will tell you now, how I spent our separate summer. When I missed him, I did math. It was 9,000 miles around the earth to where he was, but it was only 7,900 miles through the earth.

Armed with that math, I marched through a field to the lowest part of the valley, and I pressed my face and chest to the ground, my heart beating into the dirt. It was the closest I could get to him. Some days I drove past his old dorm – the room where he used to sleep and study biochemistry and pray (on his knees, no less!). He wasn't there anymore, but just seeing the window brought a sense of comfort.

That's how it felt to be in Israel. While God's Spirit lives inside of me, Israel was the closest I could get to the physical, tangible aspects of my Savior. I began to miss Him more. I longed for Him in a way that pulled on me like weights on chains. I never wanted to leave.

On our first night in Jerusalem, I sat on the roof of my hotel and wrote in my journal:

Papa, thank You for using my earthly mother and father to bring me here to fall more deeply in love with my You, my Heavenly Father. I feel like I understand You better after being here – like a kid who finally got to see the homeland her parents always talked about. It means everything to me that You chose to share this experience with me.

Jesus, please come back soon. If I have to leave this place, You have to come back. I can't be away from You. I know You're everywhere, but this place ... this nearness. Please. Come quickly, Lord Jesus.

—

Lush rolling hills and gardenia bushes surround the perimeter of the Sea of Galilee. It is more like a lake than a sea. If you stand at the north end, you can see all the way across the furthest distance. I've never been good with Biblical geography, but Galilee was miniscule compared to my imagination. I could hold all of it in my field of vision – two miles wide and five miles long.

Jesus spent the majority of His three-year ministry on and around this lake. What one Man did and said in roughly 10 square miles nearly 2,000 years ago has changed all of creation for eternity. His reach extended around the world and across millennia to me.

—

On the morning of our last full day in Israel, I shuffled through the chairs and tables, aiming for the Greek yogurt and granola. My routine breakfast in Israel felt so decadent compared to the protein smoothies I typically had back home.

I saw him approaching me as I was almost to the "Healthy Start" section of the buffet – my bus pastor, Paul, a fit, graying man who sat in the row ahead of me on the bus every day. I looked past his shoulder at the buffet awaiting me. I could smell the honey from ten feet away.

"I think God told me something about you today in my quiet time," he said, smiling, bouncing lightly on his heels. Decked out in running gear, headphones hanging around his neck, he was still sweaty from a run. He'd probably been up since the time I fell asleep.

"Oh?" Everything slowed. Suddenly the fresh local figs piled high in a glass bowl didn't matter. "What did He say?" I asked.

"Your Father said ..." Paul stopped bouncing and his face broke into a wide grin, "... that He is really pleased with you."

Tears pooled in my eyes. "Wow. Thank you. Anything else?" I asked. "Anything about His plans for Jesus to return like, today-ish?"

He laughed. "Unfortunately, no. He talked to me about you for a while, though. I tried to write a lot of it down, but that's the overall theme. Maybe I'll tell you someday, but now isn't the time."

This thing I knew to be true, the thing Scripture says is true of all of God's children, that we are acceptable and righteous in His eyes because of Christ, that He doesn't just tolerate us, but that He adores us – somehow it took on so much more meaning when someone verbalized it directly to me. I could count on two fingers the number of times that had happened in my life. It meant more than I could contain in my head at one time, so I had to keep thinking about it, reveling in it.

Those words carried me all day. They framed everything I saw, every conversation I had, every thought I processed.

Your Father is really pleased with you.

Sometimes you just need to hear it.

———

That night – our final night in Israel – I waited until everyone else had fallen asleep, then I took my Bible and my red journal and I walked out to the hotel garden overlooking Jerusalem. The Old City is lit with yellow lamplight that turns the horizon gold. Summer haze kicked up the city's halo a few levels.

I opened my journal and read through all the notes I'd taken on the trip. There, on that one mountaintop, Abraham offered Isaac,

David danced before the Ark of the Covenant, Solomon built the first Temple, and Jesus paid for my sins. The penalty for our betrayal was brutal, but that was also where God revealed the shocking wonder of restoration.

Dew began to settle on the grass. I stood, held my books to my chest, and exhaled slow and long as I stared at the century-old stone walls before me. "If I die tomorrow, this isn't the last time I'll be here," I said. "Thank you for bringing me home, Papa."

REFLECTION QUESTIONS:

1. Is the word "Father" hard to reconcile with your earthly experience of fathers? Why or why not?

2. Do you tend to distance yourself from the Father, preferring other Persons of the Trinity (Jesus and the Spirit) over Him? If so, what motivates that distancing?

3. How would it change things for you if you really believed God your Father delighted in you?

7

SLOW TO ANGER

The LORD is gracious and merciful,
slow to anger and abounding in steadfast love.
Psalm 145:8

Two days before our trip ended, I accompanied a friend to a tattoo shop in Jerusalem. We arrived to find quiet, classical music, and a meticulous shop. She asked some questions of the receptionist while I thumbed through pictures on my camera. Out of the corner of my eye, I saw the front door fly open and heard the growl of a revving engine. A motorcycle pulled across the threshold and came to a stop two feet away from me.

The driver removed his helmet and gloves, dismounted, and greeted us with a friendly, "Shalom."

"This is Raj," the receptionist explained. "He owns the shop."

"And this is my parking spot," he said, smiling. "It keeps my bike from getting scratched." He patted the gas tank.

He rubbed his three-day beard and began to grind the beans for our coffee. In many places in Israel, they give you a date to eat after you finish your coffee. We began to affectionately refer to the combo as a "coffee date." I saw him reach his tattooed arm into the cabinet and pull out a box of dates.

He wanted to know why we were in Israel. "Oh, you know ... Jesus," I said as I bounced my shoulders, my token gesture of enthusiasm.

"Americans?" he asked.

"Yeah. You?"

"Palestinian, but Buddhist," he said. "You have a wonderful country. I really like America." He poured water into the bronze pot.

"You've been? That's awesome! Have you traveled a lot? Where's your favorite place in the world?" I asked.

"Hmm ... it's easier to tell you my least favorite place. I don't like Muslim countries."

"Oh? I've never been to a Muslim country. What don't you like about them?"

"They treat their women terribly. It's better to be a hedgehog than a Muslim woman. Truly. You would have a better life."

"Oh?"

He paused, pouring my coffee into a tiny bronze mug, then continued, "In Buddhism, we believe in reincarnation, you know? So – how do I say this? I think the most gracious and kind thing you can do for a Muslim is to help speed along their process of reincarnation."

My eyes grew wide. I sipped the coffee, even though it was still too hot, just to give me a moment to think.

My friend spoke up, "You mean ...?"

"Killing them," he said, "is an act of mercy."

The strangest part was that his tone wasn't malicious or bitter. In the framework of his religion, even one that professed peace and unity among all living things, he believed murder was generous.

I wanted to talk to him longer, to ask him more questions, but we had to catch the bus to meet our tour group. I couldn't stop replaying the conversation in my head. I kept thinking how different Raj's approach was from God's approach.

The Lord is slow to anger and abounding in steadfast love, forgiving iniquity and transgression, but He will by no means clear the guilty.... - Numbers 14:18

Two common worldviews wrongly present God as only loving or only just. They attempt to disassociate the two from each other, refusing to believe He could be both. Numbers 14 says He is both of those things, and it also tells us He is slow to anger. Even in His justice, He is patient.

In Christ, I aim to model that slow anger with others. I hope to reveal His character to a world that doesn't know or understand Him. Even as I pray, "Come quickly, Lord Jesus," I follow it with, "But until You do, I'll keep asking You to reach more people with the freedom of Your love."

In Aramaic, the language Jesus likely spoke, those two prayers can be uttered in two words: "Maranatha (Come, Lord Jesus). Hosanna (Save now)."

So I pray: *Maranatha. Hosanna.*

Then, because I am not as patient as He is: *Maranatha, maranatha, maranatha.*

REFLECTION QUESTIONS:

1. Do you tend to focus on one aspect of God's character to the exclusion of others? Do you focus more on love, justice, or something else?

2. What are some dangers of not viewing God holistically and

understanding the fullness of His character? Practically, how might a partial view of God affect the way you live?

3. When have you noticed God being slow to anger toward you?

8

GRACIOUS

*For from His fullness we have all received,
grace upon grace.*
John 1:16

Raicheal and Meghann, two of my housemates in South Carolina, picked me up at the airport when I landed back in the US. I threw my arms around them awkwardly – Raicheal is taller than me, and Meghann is shorter than everyone, which made for an imbalanced group hug. Meghann scooted up into the driver's seat of her SUV as Raicheal lifted my bags into the trunk.

"Do you want me to stop so we can get you something to eat? Four or five things to drink, perhaps?" Meghann asked.

"Oh, it's so good to be known," I said, laughing. The two of them regularly teased me about how many beverages I always seemed to have on hand. Usually some combination of fruit water, yerba mate, a green smoothie, and black coffee.

The three of us had been living together for a year at Butler Manor – that's what we called our sprawling, historic house on Butler Avenue in downtown Greenville. In that two-story house with a front porch swing and a balcony, we each had our own apartments but shared a large foyer. It afforded us privacy and community in all the right proportions. We each tucked keys to our apartments into a hiding spot under the table runner in the lobby, granting ourselves full access to each others' lives whenever we pleased. We hung out several nights a week in Meghann's apartment, sitting on the hardwood floor, eating air-popped popcorn, and watching "The Voice."

That living situation was nothing less than God's grace to me; having Meghann and Raicheal as housemates was grace upon grace.

Meghann was the mom of our household, even though she's the youngest of us all. She worked as a third shift nurse in the neonatal intensive care unit, so we took all our medical questions to her. She also knew how to throw the perfect party, not missing any detail from the themed menu to the accompanying decor. I wasn't sure how she pulled it off, but she even seemed capable of controlling the weather on days when she'd planned an outdoor event. More than anything, she was a woman of prayer. Hardly a day passed without her sitting someone down, putting a soft hand on their shoulder and talking to God about what was happening in their life.

On the drive home from the airport, I felt my heart relax just being around them again. "All I want to do is move to Israel. Do you think we can find a Butler Manor in Jerusalem and all move in together there?"

"I'll drink to that," Raicheal said, lifting her Barq's into the air.

I raised an empty hand, fingers curved around an invisible cup.

"That reminds me – let's get you some beverages," Meghann said, exiting the interstate and turning on her signal light for the drive-thru Starbucks. "I'm surprised you're not dehydrated already."

Upon arriving home, I unpacked my bags and came across the souvenirs I'd bought for each of them. Meghann had left for work, but Raicheal sat on the lobby couch and squealed with delight as I handed her the porcelain bowl I'd gotten her. She radiates a joy so dense it feels like it should be fake, like she thickened it with corn starch and xanthan gum. But when it sits, viscous and undiluted, in a Friday afternoon rainstorm, my skepticism fades. She knows things I have yet to learn – the kinds of things I never cared about until her words poured out. *"And that's how we made our own bread,"* and *"Of all the countries I've lived in …"* She tells these stories without an ounce of pretension.

My heart was still heavy from leaving Israel, and I needed a beautiful story to hold my attention and revive my spirit.

So I asked her to talk. "Tell me your life story," I said. It felt like cheating. Did she know I was auditing the class she teaches? I paid no tuition. But learning her taught me more about the gentle strength I wanted to hold, with even hands. For so much knowledge, so much living, she had an easy heart.

—

God gives His children all good eternal things, and His earthly gifts point us to those eternal gifts. Living at Butler Manor with women who loved The Lord pointed my heart back to Him, the Giver of all good things. While I knew it was only a season that would pass, as all earthly things do, I took every opportunity to thank Him for it. Grace upon grace.

REFLECTION QUESTIONS:

1. What gifts in your life show God's grace to you?

2. What people in your life ask you good questions, make you feel known, and remind you of God's love for you?

3. If you don't have people like that in your life, in what ways could you seek to be that kind of person to someone else this week?

4. In what ways do you resist being known? What things are you trying to hide? What might happen (good, bad, or neutral) if you were honest? Is it worth the risk?

9
BLESSED HOPE

For the grace of God has appeared, bringing salvation for all people, training us to renounce ungodliness and worldly passions, and to live self-controlled, upright, and godly lives in the present age, waiting for our blessed hope, the appearing of the glory of our great God and Savior Jesus Christ…
Titus 2:11-13

The thing that caught me most off guard upon my return from Israel was my total inability to function. I had never felt so displaced.

Israel wasn't a mission trip. I didn't go and see impoverished people dying in makeshift hospitals filled with gurneys. I didn't dig wells or give anyone malaria medication. I made no difference in anyone's life.

Here's what I did: I cashed in a promise my dad made me. I slept well in a hotel bed, I ate decadent foods in a city of luxury and beauty. Yet I could hardly hold myself together after I got back. I didn't know what was happening to my heart. All my self-analyzing skills were failing me.

It wasn't despair or depression, just a deep longing. It wasn't an unnamed, nebulous one – it was precise. It made itself known with a lump in my throat and a quivering lower lip. If I could boil it down to a smooth reduction, it would have one note: *I want Him back. Now.*

I tried, but I couldn't get my heart to land in the present for long. I prayed and fasted for His return. I wanted to tell everyone I knew to beg Him with me. *"Maybe if we just band together,"* I thought, *"He'll give in and get a move on."* I was soul-weary to the deepest parts of me. I even wrote a song about it, begging Him. The chorus says:

Would You bend a holy ear
To hear a sinner's tune?
Every heart is singing
Would You come back soon?
Come back soon.

As I drove to my women's Discipleship Group on Monday night, the sky was lit up like a campfire – red and warm and radiant. I kept looking, hoping He would break through the clouds.

One of the first things we do at D-Group each week is split off into separate rooms with our prayer partner to share our requests and pray over each other. My prayer partner for that series was Jenn, a feisty grad student with long dark curls.

For the past few months, she had been experiencing a lot of health struggles like migraines and vision loss, which kept her out of college for the semester. Sharing my feelings about Israel seemed so emotional and needy in light of all she had endured, but one of the things I loved about D-Group was that we could be honest about where we were struggling, without fear.

As the other girls paired off in different corners of the apartment, Jenn and I grabbed our pens and notepads and headed to our usual spot in the adirondack chairs on the balcony.

"It seems so frustrating and inefficient to ache for Him while He's just taking His sweet time," I told her. "He shows every sign of coming back, but then pauses. It's like He's got His hand on the reins, the horse's hoof in the air, poised and ready ... And I'm here with one eye on the clock and one on the sky. Does this sound weird? Am I being artsy or hyper-spiritual or totally unrelatable?"

"No, I get it," she said. "In the past year, if there's anything I have felt an increased longing for, it's His return. With all this pain I've been having, and none of the doctors knowing how to fix me, He is the only answer."

"I know that none of us really knows how it's going to go down in the end. All I know for sure is that He said He's coming back, and that it's going to be 'soon.' People always think it's happening in their time, but someone has to be right eventually."

"Better to err on the side of hope, I suppose," she said.

"But what do I do in the meantime?"

"The homeless shelter that I volunteer at — one of the guys who works there always says he's just trying to do what he can only do now."

"What do you mean?"

"Well, do the things that won't be necessary or possible once He comes back. For now, you can keep making disciples and listening to broken hearts. For now, you can feed the needy. For now, you can speak hope and encouragement, you can help people see their potential for His glory. You will never again get to do those things once He comes back and restores it all."

"Jenn, I think you just changed everything for me. I've got to do something with this longing. And that's the only thing that makes any sense. After all, it's what He said to do with it."

In the midst of my desire for Him, I had lost sight of His commands to me.

If we hope for what we do not see, we wait for it with patience. - Romans 8:25

I wouldn't consider myself an overly emotional person, but what I feel, I feel deeply. It's easy sometimes to let those emotions distract me from the bigger picture of my eternal hope in Him and His eternal purpose for me.

How sweet of Him to send gentle reminders instead of rebukes, at a time when I felt weak with longing for Him. I was a bruised reed, in the words of the prophet Isaiah, and He did not break me.

REFLECTION QUESTIONS:

1. What earthly things do you hope for?

2. What eternal / Kingdom things do you hope for?

3. In Matthew 6:21, Jesus said, "Where your treasure is, there you heart will be also." How does that verse challenge you? Be specific.

4. What are some practical ways you can fix your heart on working toward Kingdom things today, instead of laying up earthly treasures?

10

SAVIOR

The Son of Man came to seek and to save the lost. - Luke 19:10

If God is sovereign, why should we pray about anything? Why should we tell other people about Jesus at all?

I think it's kind of like this: God is your Provider, but usually the means by which He provides is through you having a job. It's the same thing with prayer and evangelism – we get to be tools in His hand to accomplish His will.

One morning, not long after I got back from Israel, I took my Bible and a cup of green tea with coconut milk to the balcony at the front of our house. I propped my feet up, watching joggers dodge the low-hanging magnolias, stroller moms talking on bluetooths, and homeless men wearing too many clothes for the heat of an August day in South Carolina. The alarm of a Smart Car went off across the street; it sounded like a hummingbird.

I opened my journal and looked down at the page where I had written the words Jenn spoke to me at D-Group: *"Do what you can only do now."*

Beneath that, I drew a line and wrote: "What can only be done now?" I listed off a few things – take improv comedy classes, tour Europe, run another race – but it started to feel like I was making a bucket list. It all just seemed so … temporary.

I drew another line and wrote: "What eternal things can only be done now?" It didn't even take me a second to know what belonged in that category. I immediately wrote beneath it: "Share the Gospel with Anna."

Anna was my hair stylist. From the moment I first sat in her chair a year earlier, I felt like God was after her heart, like He deeply loved her. By all appearances, she was rough around the edges – her short, spiky hair changed colors weekly, she wore four-inch, platform heels throughout all three of her pregnancies, and she had multiple visible tattoos. But sometimes soft hearts make themselves known in other ways – like the way she teared up when I told stories about God, the questions she asked me, the texts she sent me after she read my memoir, *Orange Jumpsuit*.

"I want what you have," she texted me, the day after I gave her a copy of the book. "I see it and I want it."

"What do you mean?" I asked.

"The God stuff. I want to know Him like that."

My heart quickened. My eyes filled with tears. I typed so fast my phone could barely keep up.

"Do you want to talk about it? Can I come over?"

I went to Anna's apartment that night. She let her kids stay up past their bedtimes, and I played with them until after midnight. I wanted them to know Jesus, too. So every time I held them or wiped a nose or loaded a spoon with Cheerios, I begged God to draw them near, clean them up, feed them from His hand. *Pleasepleaseplease,* I prayed.

After the kids fell asleep, Anna pulled the strings on her hoodie, tucked her feet up under her legs, making her tiny body look even smaller.

"How did you get to this place where you are?" she asked.

"Me? Honestly? He dragged me here," I laughed. "The truth is: I am not good enough to want Him on my own. I want bad things. Even still, sometimes."

"Whatever. You're like, the perfect Christian."

"No. I promise you. Not just in big things, but in stupid little things, too. I can't even get the small things right sometimes."

"Like what?"

"Like ..." I widened my eyes and threw my head back, "Sometimes I want to steal rolls of toilet paper when I go into fancy restrooms." I clenched both fists in the air and shook them, defeated. "Aaaaagh!"

She laughed, then put on a forced stern face. "Stay out of my salon bathroom."

"You've been warned," I said. "But seriously, the story of 'how I got to this place' is that I just felt Him pulling at my heart. I feel it still, everyday. He's so persistent. Is that kind of like what you feel?"

"Yes. I just know I can't do this on my own," she said. "That's hard for me to admit, because I feel like I can do everything on my own. I'm a single mom, I run my own business. For crying out loud, I was cutting a client's hair when my water broke during my first pregnancy, and I finished the cut!"

"Whoa!"

"But I just know I need Him."

"This resonates with me," I said. "I feel the same way sometimes. My independence tries to fool me. I'm not as self-sufficient as I'd like to believe. It's humbling, isn't it?"

"Yeah. Kind of the opposite of what all the self help books teach."

I nodded and sat up straight. "Hey, do you want to come to church with me on Sunday?"

It felt like a copout. I once heard a pastor say: "If you want someone to be religious, take them to church. If you want them to be saved, take them to Jesus." That made a lot of sense to me, but inviting her to my church just seemed like the right thing to do at the time.

"Yes!" she said. She sat up straight and put her hand to her chest, delighted.

I beamed. "Okay then!"

We settled on a time, and I told her to wear whatever she felt comfortable in. On Sunday, I halfway expected a text telling me she couldn't make it – not because of anything she said, but because of my own insecurities about inviting people to church.

On Sunday, she came, and she took notes.

—

Thud thump thump draaaaaag thumpthumpthump.

Through my earplugs, I could hear the noises. I pulled my eye mask off and took the earplugs out. Time for my daily game of "Determine the Origin of that Noise." So far the options I'd come up with were: visitor with a poorly chosen knocking pattern, squirrels on the roof, a murderer sneaking through attic.

I picked up the broom, stood on my bed, and thwacked the 10' ceiling with the wooden end. The noises stopped, but by that point I was fully awake. *Might as well start the day,* I thought. *I've even got time for a run before church.*

While I was out running, I got a text from Anna. It had been a few weeks since she first came to church with me, and I'd been out of town on tour during the Sundays that followed.

I read the text while shuffling down the trail. "Can I go to church with you again today? I really liked it. My dad is in town and he wants to come, too."

We slid into the end of an aisle near the back. The room was full, the congregation already standing to sing. During the service, Anna grew fidgety. Crossing her right leg over her left, then vice versa, tucking her hair under her cap. Her dad sat to her right, perfectly still.

At the end of the service, my pastor stood and said, "As I've been talking, there are some of you who have reached the conclusion that you can't do this on your own." I wanted to look at Anna, but I just kept my eyes forward and begged Him. *Pleasepleaseplease.*

He continued, "If you feel like your heart is about to come out of your chest – that's God, drawing you in. That's Him calling you to come home right now. If you want to come home to Him, will you just stand up where you are right now? There's nothing magic about standing up – it's just a visible way to acknowledge you're responding to His work in your heart right now."

Pleasepleaseplease.

Anna's left hand, covered in music note tattoos, grabbed my right hand. She squeezed. I saw her looking at me, and I turned to face her. Underneath the brim of her hat, tears spilled down her face. She pressed her lips together and nodded.

I stood with her. I wrapped my arms around her, overjoyed.

God had said *yesyesyes* to my *pleasepleaseplease*.

I remember how He rescued me. It does my heart good to acknowledge it – He saved me from a life of alcoholism and drug abuse and rampant fornication – at the age of four. He saved me from hopelessness and from the failed legalistic pursuit of my own righteousness.

Don't let the age of my conversion fool you into thinking I was innocent or that I only barely needed Him. Those of us who share the testimony of a childhood conversion were born with the same black heart and the same sin nature as those who meet Him in prisons and brothels. He is no less a Savior to those of us who were adopted young as to those who are adopted out of deathbeds. We all need Him just the same. Downplaying your testimony diminishes the saving work of Christ on your behalf.

When I forget that He saved me, or even just that He saves at all, it's easy for me to be distracted by temporary things. I sat in Anna's chair for two years, talking about boys and tattoos and the new restaurants in town. Those aren't bad conversations to have, but they aren't valuable either. In the mere month I spent actively praying for her and sharing Christ with her, everything changed.

The saying is trustworthy and deserving of full acceptance, that Christ Jesus came into the world to save sinners, of whom I am the foremost. - 1 Timothy 1:15

He sought me when I was far from Him. He found me. He saved me.

I rejoiced to see Him do the same for Anna. I wonder how much greater is my rejoicing over her salvation, having sown prayers and tears and conversations toward this answer? How generous of Him to use sinners as tools in the saving of other sinners. How blessed I was to be a tool in His hand.

REFLECTION QUESTIONS:

1. Where were you in your life when He saved you? How have you seen His redemption play out in your life since then?

2. If you were young or particularly "morally upright" (i.e. "a good person") when He saved you, have you ever been tempted to diminish your need for His salvation? If so, how can you reframe this to align with the truth?

3. Who has God given you a burden to share the Gospel with? If you don't have a burden to share the Gospel, do you really believe it?

11

MERCIFUL

...Let us fall into the hand of The LORD, for His mercy is great.
2 Samuel 24:14

Every three months, I fly to Arizona to lead worship at a multi-site church. Building relationships with people through repeated events is one of the blessings of my line of work.

I picked up my rental car at Sky Harbor Airport and headed to the hotel, excited to see my far-away church family again at rehearsal that night. The speed limit was 75, but no one was abiding by it. I pulled an apple out of my purse, rolled down the windows, and turned up the radio as I headed toward Phoenix. The dry Arizona heat was a nice change from South Carolina's humidity.

I passed several cars. Eventually I checked my odometer. The rental company was out of economy cars and had given me a Mustang instead. Without even feeling it, I was cruising at nearly 100 miles per hour. Oops. I slowed to 90, which somehow seemed like crawling. The road was as smooth and effortless as a water slide.

Suddenly, it felt like God spoke to me: *Do not pass the purple minivan.*

What a strange thing to say, God, I thought.

Then it felt like the voice came back again, insistent. *Do not pass the purple minivan.*

I'd been passing everything, but okay. In case it was God speaking, I decided to obey. I passed every car between me and the purple minivan, which was also speeding, and pulled in behind it, still doing 85.

The instant I caught up to the minivan, we drove under an overpass. Hidden on the other side was a state trooper. He pulled out, threw on his lights. My heart raced. I slowed and pulled over, watching as the state trooper passed me to chase down the purple minivan.

In my hotel room that night, I thought about the incident for a long time, trying to figure out why God would spare me the punishment for my actions. I had been speeding. God could've kept quiet and let me get the ticket I deserved, but He didn't. Instead, He saved me from the consequences of my sins.

He has a history of doing this, of drawing near to sinners in the midst of their rebellion and offering a substitute to take the punishment they deserve. In my mind, the purple minivan was a sort of Christ-type, who took what I deserved. The analogy fell apart a little, since the minivan was speeding / sinning, and Christ never did that. But still, I felt God's mercy toward me in the midst of my own sin.

One of my mentors loves to drive that point home to me whenever my life isn't going like I prayed it would, and I begin to wonder if God might be punishing me for some sin I committed: "You will never ever ever ever ever see the wrath of God. Never ever. On the cross, Christ absorbed the Father's wrath for all of His children. So if you are His child, you will not see His wrath. Never ever ever."

The discipline He gives is only given out of grace, to call us back into fellowship. That's why, as my pastor Matt Chandler says, those who understand the gospel can run *to* God when they sin, while those who don't understand the gospel run *from* Him when they sin.

Watching God spare me of the penalty of my sin, even in something as small as a speeding ticket, painted a bigger picture of His character for me. I had a tangible story of what His mercy looked like.

When He is gracious, He gives me what I don't deserve; when He is merciful, He does not give me what I do deserve. Both His grace and His mercy reveal that I am needy and incapable, and both point me to a God who is infinitely generous.

God, being rich in mercy, because of the great love with which He loved us, even when we were dead in our trespasses, made us alive together with Christ ... By grace you have been saved through faith. And this is not your own doing; it is the gift of God, not a result of works, so that no one may boast. - Ephesians 2:4-5, 9-10

REFLECTION QUESTIONS:

1. What are some specific ways God has shown you mercy and spared you from the consequences of your sins?

2. If you were talking to someone who didn't know The Lord, how would you describe the Spirit's prompting of conviction to keep you from sin? What does it feel like to you or what happens in your thoughts?

3. When you sin, do you run to God or from Him? Why?

12

MASTER

No servant can serve two masters, for either he will hate the one and love the other, or he will be devoted to the one and despise the other.
You cannot serve God and money.
Luke 16:13

Jeannie fit perfectly at Butler Manor. She moved into the second bedroom in my upstairs apartment to join our little community for a few months before getting married.

Living with a bunch of single girls has the potential to be stressful, but somehow we managed to turn Butler Manor into a place where people felt nurtured. Meghann, Raicheal, Jeannie, and I spent autumn evenings in the white adirondack rockers on the wood-plank front porch, swatting at mosquitoes and stinkbugs, cooling the night with homemade sangria. We took walks through our neighborhood downtown, beneath low-hanging boughs draped in twinkle lights. Magnolia and jasmine filled the air.

Between Meghann's sewing skills and Jeannie's knack for finding charming thrift store bargains, we helped Jeannie plan a wedding that would thrill both Dave Ramsey and Martha Stewart. We even picked up some things to add designer touches to our apartment.

One day while Jeannie was at work, I drove to the store to return a $7 pair of king size pillowcases, because they were too large. They had been marked down 50% when I bought them. The large size, which I needed instead, were still full price at $14. I fought with God the whole way there, because I wanted to return my $7 ones, go to the display, and switch the packaging before buying the large ones (in the king size packaging).

No. You're not going to do that, is what I sensed the Spirit saying.

"Why do I have to pay more for less fabric? That doesn't even make sense." I questioned.

This is not open for discussion, came the reply.

The more I'm actively working to be aware of God's presence, to remember He is always present with me, the more He produces a reverence in me that protects me from making foolish, sinful decisions. Familiarity with Him brings the awe and delight of "the fear of The Lord." It makes me want to know Him better, to delight in Him even more fully.

As I stood in the aisles of the home goods store, I thought of His mercy to me when I was speeding across Arizona. Remembering that incident made me delight in Him. A passage of Scripture popped into my head.

Trust in The Lord with all your heart,
and do not lean on your own understanding.
In all your ways acknowledge Him,
and He will make straight your paths.
- Proverbs 3:5-6

Rationalizing about the cost of fabric per square inch certainly counted as "leaning on my own understanding." Ignoring the Spirit's prompting would not count as "acknowledging Him." As much as I wanted to do what I wanted, I wanted even more to be obedient to His commands.

I preached the gospel to myself in the linens aisle. *"I delight in You more than in pillow cases. I delight in You more than $7."* It was a pretty basic gospel, but exactly what I needed to remember at the time.

While driving home after paying the full $14 for my size large pillow cases, I realized I almost sold God out for a difference of $7. I almost betrayed the only one who loves me unconditionally – and who would've loved me still, had I done it – for the cost of a matinee movie.

—

I felt the need to confess my evil desires, even though I didn't act on them, to my D-Group, which included all of my housemates. It may sound extreme, but I wanted us to start dealing with heart issues before they manifested in our actions. I longed to live in a culture of repentance and confession and healing – like God talks about in James 5:16. As the D-Group leader, I knew I needed to lead the way in helping create that culture.

After I confessed, they laughed nervously, maybe to comfort me, but they didn't diminish or excuse my sin. I looked around our living room at the women I led each week, and I knew we had something real. Being honest with D-Group about my sin somehow made me feel more loved, like oil was being poured over me. My whole body warmed.

Because of the way He loves so well, I see the deep beauty in confession and openness. If we insist on trying to maintain a moral image, we lose access to one of the main ways we can deal a blow to the enemy. Public confession and repentance are powerful weapons of our warfare. When we bring our whole selves forward in vulnerability, and the Body of Christ responds with gentleness and comfort, we demonstrate Christ's victory in the battle.

I used to think obedience was primarily the way I showed God I love Him, but John 14:21 says obedience is also a means for me to feel God's love for me, not just demonstrate my love for Him. I felt it from His Spirit and from His people – the great love that Luke 6:35 says is kind, even to the ungrateful and the evil.

He is the Master, but He is a kind one. Becoming who He is making me into means He gets to do the shaping, while I do the yielding. It means surrender to the better and more beautiful thing I may not yet have eyes to see.

Behold, as the eyes of servants look to the hand of their master, as the eyes of a maidservant to the hand of her mistress, so our eyes look to The Lord our God, 'til He has mercy upon us. - Psalm 123:2

REFLECTION QUESTIONS:

1. Describe a time when you responded to God as your Master, obeying His promptings.

2. Describe a time when you leaned on your own understanding or did not acknowledge Him as Master?

3. Have you ever resisted prayer, fearing God might say something you didn't want to hear? What does that fear reveal about your view of God?

4. What might be some positive side effects of confession within community?

5. Do you have people to walk out James 5:16 with?

13
PORTION

My flesh and my heart may fail,
but God is the strength of my heart and my portion forever.
Psalm 73:26

Was there sleep before the fall? I wonder if, in the new heaven, there will be sleep. And if so, surely even our dreams are redeemed.

For now my dreams consist primarily of some unspoken goal I can't accomplish. Usually, I'm trying to get somewhere but am thwarted at every turn.

Last night I encountered a series of obstacles: trying to find things I had lost (my notebook, my car), trying to do something I'd forgotten to do (give a series of talks I failed to write), and trying to use various forms of transportation which all ended up failing me (the ship capsized, the flight was cancelled, the highway had been destroyed, leaving only chunks of blacktop piled behind construction barriers).

No dream is rest, no dream leaves me relishing the perfection. Unlike some dreamers, I never stretch my arms wide and fly. All of my life, even my dream life, feels like a collection of assignments I keep botching, coupled with desires I invariably am denied.

I love His promise that I won't be chasing things forever, always coming up empty-handed. One day, the only Thing I've ever really wanted will be always mine.

—

"Tara-Leigh! I don't know why I didn't think of this before. I know the perfect man for you!"

The text from my married friend came on a morning when she had no idea how much I needed it. I'd had a dream a few hours earlier, where I'd shown up at my own wedding and the groom was nowhere to be found. I woke frantic and angst-ridden.

My friend and her husband, along with another married couple I know, conspired to set me up with a man they deemed a great fit, and she was texting me to gauge my interest level. On paper, this guy was the real deal. He was a small group leader at his church, had a high-level job in engineering, and had even done some modeling. It took them every bit of 30 seconds to convince me to meet him.

They threw a party, ostensibly to introduce us. As the days approached, they suggested we become friends on Facebook. We started talking. Not much, just enough to help me feel relaxed about meeting him. He made me laugh with his quick wit, and he even laughed at the poorly-constructed jokes I second-guessed.

When the night of the party came, I was excited to finally feel open. For the first time since Joel, I felt the hint of the possibility of hope. I arrived at the party and realized I only knew a few people there. I stood in the archway separating the living room from the patio, talking to one of the wives. He approached with two glasses of water, handing one of them to me. He didn't even know me, but he was already meeting my high-demand beverage consumption needs. Considerate? Check. Handsome? Check.

Throughout the night I found out more impressive things about him. For instance, he graduated from an Ivy League school, where he also rowed crew. His family had a crest, for crying out loud. He was like a thoroughbred. For that reason, I will call him Seabiscuit.

Seabiscuit and I talked well into the night, and at the end of the party, he asked if he could drive me home. Ever the gentleman, he held all the doors, requested my number, and called the next day to ask me out on a proper date. There was no second-guessing his intentions. The way he treated me – and everyone he encountered, for that matter – conveyed the way he valued people. It reflected Christ.

My friends were right. This guy was a catch.

—

The day of our date arrived. I had never been so nervous before a date in all my life. I even called a friend to come help me with my hair, because I kept dropping the flat iron, and I was afraid I would end up with questionable burns on my face. I imagined it: *Tara-Leigh, is that a hickey on your forehead?*

One of the wives of the couples who set us up texted me half an hour before he picked me up. "Just be careful. Lots of girls like him and fall for him hard. Keep your head on straight."

You're not helping! I thought, as I zipped up my knee-high winter boots, teetering and stumbling. I steadied myself at the edge of my bed and tossed the phone onto my pillow. The screen lit up again, and I leaned over to read it.

"Have fun with Seabiscuit!" the other wife texted. "Can't wait to hear how it goes!"

On our date, he loosely planned the series of events, constructing them around my preferences. He asked meaningful questions. He paid for everything quickly, so I didn't have to wonder what my role was.

He should probably write a book on how to respectfully date a woman.

Despite his near-flawless interaction with me, I wasn't the least bit interested in him. At the end of the night, I sat perched on the end of my bed, beating myself up in my head.

Why don't I like him? What is wrong with me? If I can't like this guy, I'm doomed.

My friends encouraged me to give it another try, so I did. The second date was even more frustrating than the first. After I got home, I put my hair up in a topknot, made some tea, and called one of the wives.

"Well, that settles it," I said. "I'm going to die alone." I shuffled from the kitchen into my bedroom, tea in one hand, phone in the other.

She laughed. "Whatever! Just because you don't like him doesn't mean there isn't someone for you."

I set the tea on my nightstand, put her on speakerphone, and threw myself back on my bed.

"No, it's okay," I said. "I'm certain marriage is awesome, but on the bright side, I sure do love only making one side of the bed." I rolled over onto my side and stuffed a pillow under my arm, propping myself up.

"Tara-Leigh. Stop being ridiculous."

"My positive takeaway from this is that I was able to be excited about it. Even if it fell flat, it just feels good to be hopeful again."

"There's someone out there for you."

I resisted the urge to roll my eyes. "Look," I said, "I appreciate the gesture, honestly. But that's not necessarily true. God hasn't promised me that. He hasn't promised any of us tomorrow, much less husbands. I don't need false hope – I need hope in the real thing. Otherwise I end up getting angry when He doesn't fulfill those things He never promised me anyway."

"I hear you," she said. "I just don't want you to lose hope. Marriage is a good thing to desire."

I thought about David. He wanted to build the Temple for God. God told David it was an honorable desire, a good thing to want. God didn't say it was bad or wrong, but He told David no. *David*. The man after God's own heart.

God cares about how hopeful we are, because our level of hope shows how much we know His Word, trust His character, walk in His strength. Romans 15 says that hope is one of the reasons Scripture exists. But He also cares about what our hope is in. I don't need to have hope for marriage. I need to have hope in God. That will carry me through whatever He has for me – marriage or singleness or sudden death.

Maybe my dreams will always feel a little too much like real life, never easy or beautiful. Maybe my desire for marriage is like David with his Temple blueprints in hand. Maybe marriage is my good desire, but one that will only be fulfilled in eternity, where I'm part of the Bride of Christ. If that's the case, there is no less joy for me. He always has been and always will be enough. He is enough for my contentment. He is enough for my fullness. No matter what else He puts on my plate, He is more than enough.

The LORD is my chosen portion and my cup; You hold my lot. The lines have fallen for me in pleasant places; indeed, I have a beautiful inheritance. - Psalm 16:5-6

REFLECTION QUESTIONS:

1. Does it ever feel like God is not enough?

2. What other things do you look for to be your portion?

3. What false hopes have failed you?

4. Why is putting your hope in God an effort that never fails?

14

LORD OF HOSTS

*He will command His angels concerning you
to guard you in all your ways.
Psalm 91:11*

I don't run to win, I run to finish. Maybe I should mention first that I'm not supposed to run at all. The doctors told me not to, because I was born with three heart conditions, two of which are serious, and which they say will require me to undergo open-heart surgery at some point in the future.

I run anyway. In part, because I feel like God compels me to. By His grace, I've never had an injury or even a close call. I've even done extreme things like train for and run a half marathon while doing a 40-day fast, run entire races without even a day of training, and race on zero sleep without stretching. Foolish, I know, but He has been so kind despite my foolishness.

I'm not fast, but I have always finished. The first race I wanted to quit was my fourth race, the Reedy River 10K. The course was a downtown loop past my house, which would've made quitting easy and shameless. There was an older man, probably 45 years old, who was pacing with me the whole time. He had the physique and form of an elite runner, so I wasn't sure why he was moving at my pace. Maybe an injury?

Sometimes I got a bit ahead of him, but he never dropped far behind. Once, I stopped to tie my shoe and saw him look over his shoulder to make sure I was okay. He slowed until I caught up with him.

Around Mile 4, when we were on a long hill, the rain started coming down pretty heavy. My shoes were soaked, and I just wanted to rip off my number, stash it in a trash can, and walk home, but I kept going because he was there. I started to feel like he was my pace angel. We kept steady until the end, never even speaking. Crossing the finish, I was right in front of him. I turned to take a picture of the finish line crowds and to thank him for keeping me in the race, but he wasn't there. I looked for him at the water station afterward, and I even scanned my picture for him later, but he was nowhere to be found.

My fifth race was a night race. I hadn't trained at all, but I had been running 3-4 miles per day. Somewhere between Miles 5 and 6, I was trudging uphill and hating it. Fortunately, I had my headphones in, and my favorite song of all time, Coldplay's "Fix You," was on. It gave me some added endorphins.

It was a split-road race, out and back, so I was running far to the right side of the road. Then I heard a man behind me, just over my right shoulder, say something in a fairly loud voice, which was clear even over Coldplay.

"I'm really proud of you. Well done. I'm really proud of you."

It seemed so personal. I turned to see who it was. I had come to run the race alone, but maybe a friend spotted me?

No one was there.

What do I make of these two instances? Angels? Maybe. I don't know. I'd like to think so. After all, Hebrews 1:14 says they are "ministering spirits sent out to serve for the sake of those who are to inherit salvation."

Maybe He gives me special moments of grace in these times, because of the risks I'm taking to run. Or maybe He just wants to be sweet to His children. Scripture is filled with angels, speaking God's love and His plan to His people. He's the God of all His angels – *the Lord of Hosts* – sending them on mission among humanity to point back to Him and His glory.

I may never know who those men were. But even amidst the question, and regardless of the answer, I cry out: Glory to God.

REFLECTION QUESTIONS:

1. Have you ever had an unexplained encounter like the one described here?

2. How do angels glorify The Lord in their interaction with His followers?

3. In Scripture, angels never receive worship, but always point back to God instead. How has media skewed our Biblical understanding of the role of angels?

15

SOURCE

Godliness with contentment is great gain, for we brought nothing into the world, and we cannot take anything out of the world.
1 Timothy 6:6-7

My best friend Lauren is an actress and vocalist who lives in a third-floor walk-up in the East Village. She shares the tiny space with a Ukrainian opera singer and the opera singer's violent cat who is an emotional eater. Lauren's heart-shaped face and perfect brunette ringlets land her spots in yogurt commercials and Starbucks ads, but her wholesome appearance belies her quirky Liz Lemon personality.

I texted Lauren. "I've got a four hour layover in NYC. If I take the E train from JFK, can you meet me for a hot dog after work?"

"Yes! It's been too long! Southeast corner of 53rd and 5th?"

"Perfect. It's a date. How will I even recognize you after all this time?" I asked. It had only been three months since I last saw her.

"Me? I'll be the one thinking about birds," she replied.

The round trip would take two hours, going through security again would take another hour, which gave me one hour to hang out with Lauren in the greatest city in the world, the city I had lived in for three years and never stopped loving.

—

We sat on a bench at the edge of the park, catching up on life and eating chili dogs.

"How has your week been?" I asked.

"I went on a date with a guy from church who ordered the most expensive thing on the menu, then asked me if I could pay since he was low on cash this week. You?"

"Well, I'm going to Europe in three hours."

"You win this round," she said, toasting with her half-empty paper cup. "But I still live in New York."

"Okay then, we're tied," I said. "As for men, I've got nothing. I find it almost impossible to be interested in anyone."

"Please tell me you're past the Joel thing." She looked at me sideways, her blue eyes suddenly serious.

I set my cup down on the bench. "I've been on a few dates, but I just haven't met anyone since him who interests me," I said, folding up my plate and napkin. "Maybe that was it for me. You know?"

"You could always join the new Protestant Convent I'm starting." Lauren often tried to bring levity to the conversation any time singleness came up.

"ProCon. How fitting. Sign me up."

I wondered though, was the thought of singleness a sign I had given up? Or was I just refocusing my hope? Was it resignation or contentment?

Touring launches me into nearly full-time solitude, except for the hours before, during, and after shows, when it feels like, for better or worse, I am the center of everyone's attention. I'm an extrovert, but just barely. Those times of being totally "on" mean I can subsequently spend days afterward alone, and feel no worse for the wear. Maybe even better.

I wonder if that's why people can go crazy if they're left alone in the wilderness or in solitary confinement for too long, but insanity is less of a threat if those people live alone in society. I think the madness that comes in solitude derives from the absence of God-images – that is, people. The image of God is the most beautiful thing on earth. As much as I marvel at the moon and the Horsehead Nebula, they aren't as beautiful as the eyes that fall on these pages. We desperately need the reminders of God all around us in order to function. The strange thing about thriving in solitude is it detaches me from things I deeply need, whether I know it or not.

When I started to feel content, when I started to wonder if I had wrapped up my life's final dating relationship, with all its sweetness and sadness, by making amends with Joel, then I started to feel a strange freedom. But on the heels of that freedom came worry. Contentment concerned me on a few fronts:

- Am I content because I'm selfish and don't want to have to bend my life to suit someone else? And if so, does that mean I have to get married?

- Alternately, does my contentment mean I'm supposed to be single forever? I don't want that kind of life sentence dropped on me this early in the story.

Mostly, it just felt weird. It was strange to long for no one except Jesus. He kept me busy with that for sure. Every flash of light in the sky, every sudden shadow on the ground had me throwing back my head to see if it was Him ripping the atmosphere apart. In fact, I'd never once been disappointed by the moon, except for one night when it lit up the clouds from behind and I thought, *"Now?!"* Except no, it was just the moon.

Prior to Israel, I would pray for His return when my heart was broken or life was hard and I despaired. I only wanted Him because He was better than the bad things.

But after Israel, I found myself praying for His return simply because I like Him so much. I realized: He's not just better than the bad things. He is better than the *best* things. Whenever I saw a beautiful sunset, or tasted a great steak, or laughed so hard my face hurt, I thought, *And these are just shadows! Just fractions of the fullness of joy, given to us to point us toward Him! What will it be like to feel the form, not just the shadow?*

Happiness and joy only intensified the ache, in the same way that my contentment left me ill at ease. What strange paradoxes.

Romans 11:36 says that everything is from Him and through Him and to Him. In the grand scheme of things, then, it doesn't really matter what He plans to bring me in life, because He is the source, supply, and goal of it all.

I have learned in whatever situation I am [even if the situation itself is one of uncertainty] to be content. - Philippians 4:11

I don't know if I'm supposed to be single forever or not, but I'm starting to wonder if contentment means giving up the need to have that question answered before its time. Maybe part of contentment is the willingness to bear uncertainty, to trust the Source, Supply, and Goal of my life to carry out His plan with love.

REFLECTION QUESTIONS:

1. What good desires stifle your ability to trust God as your source?

2. Have you ever forced an answer to a question, simply because you refused to be content with the timing of God's process? What was the outcome?

3. In what areas of your life might you benefit from the willingness to bear uncertainty?

16

GOOD SHEPHERD

Though I walk in the midst of trouble,
You preserve my life.
Psalm 138:7

Mom says I've been packing for travel my whole life. When I was three years old, I used to pack my own diapers and pajamas to spend the night at my grandma's house. I can live for two months out of a carry-on and a backpack, provided I stay in the same climate, and I can usually get within a few pounds of accurately guessing the weight of my luggage. These are the things touring has taught me.

When I asked my friend Emily if she wanted to tour Europe with me, it was more of a joke than an actual request. I didn't expect her to pull it off. She was the first of my housemates at Butler Manor, but since she moved out, she got a job at a doctor's office, and she barely had free time to hangout.

Much to my delight, the office gave her three weeks off work, so she was able to join me for part of my whirlwind European tour: 9 countries, 36 flights, 5 trains, 3 buses, 2 ferries, and a donkey.

Emily is the only Democrat I know who wears sweater sets and pearls. She is manicured, poised, and crazy about non-profit work. I wondered what kind of damage the suitcase life might do to her vast array of Lilly Pulitzer dresses, but she seemed up for the challenge. In fact, she managed to pack in a smaller amount of space than I did. I was impressed with her frugality.

As I prepared for the tour, I realized Italy was the only country where I would be traveling without Emily and where I didn't have an English-speaking host. I checked out some language CDs from the library to cover my bases. Learning Italian felt like gargling gumdrops. The CDs were kind of sketchy, too. They taught a conversation phrase by phrase, then when they finally strung it all together at the end, it ended up being a weird pickup line.

"Excuse me, Miss. Do you speak Italian?"

"Yes. I'm American. But I speak Italian a little."

"Your Italian is very good."

"Thank you."

"Would you like to have a drink with me later?"

"Yes. When and where?"

"Tonight. At my hotel."

No, thank you! I'm just trying to find out how to order gelato!

I also brushed up on my Spanish a little, but Emily had worked as a teacher in Mexico, so I planned to rely on her expertise where necessary. Her office job gave her enough time away to make the rounds to six countries with me: Spain, Greece, Belgium, Netherlands, England, and Germany.

Before we left, I emailed her a list of five things I'd been praying about for our trip. Some pertained to the ways I wanted to grow personally and in ministry, and others were desperate cries for Him to show up and provide. I was scheduled to play a lot of military events, and with the recent government budget cuts, many of them could only pay me a fraction of my normal rate. So I prayed for these things:

- Opportunities to minister to strangers

- Safe, on-time travel

- To live out Philippians 2:3 by serving each other well

- To love each other more at the end of the trip

- Upgrades and free things (meals, travel, etc.)

I felt pretty bold asking God for all of it, but He says to ask, and since He owns everything, it didn't seem far-fetched that He might say yes to at least some of those things. I also prayed that He would set my heart right in it – if and when any blessings came, I prayed that my first response would be praise and gratitude toward Him.

———

On the southern coast of Spain, we ate Argentine food at a seasonal pop-up restaurant built with wooden planks and beams in the sand. Cream-colored sheer curtains hung from the makeshift pergola and billowed in the wind as the sun was setting over the ocean. In Barcelona, we rented a Vespa and drove through the hills of the city, then slept in bedroom with a picture window facing La Sagrada Familia, Antoni Gaudi's unfinished basilica.

On the way to Greece, we met with unexpected adventure. There were a lot of drawbacks to visiting a country with a fledgling economy, but the upside was cheap travel. We found affordable tickets to ride the ferry from Athens to our bucket-list destination, the Greek island of Santorini. Once there, we planned to spend three days cooling in the shade of the white cave houses with blue rooftops made famous by Pinterest and the Travel Channel. A dream come true.

The eight-hour ferry ride, however, was less than dreamy. Chipped paint, water leaks, an empty (as in, waterless) deck pool, week-old bread, and drunk adults who were passed out on plastic adirondack chairs, leaving their rambunctious children free to run screaming through the hallways. Emily went to the dining room to read in peace, while I decided to run laps around the upper deck. I laced up my shoes and put in my headphones.

Halfway through my first lap, I was stopped by two men standing at the front of the boat.

"Scusi, Italiana?" the shorter one asked.

I had flashbacks of my Italian language CDs. *Uh oh.*

"No, Americana."

He threw his head back, frustrated. "Ahhhh, I always know who is Italian. I cannot believe I was wrong!"

I offered a smile and a shrug, then waved as I passed them to take another lap. They stopped me again during my next lap.

"You are a long way from home," the tall, thin one said. He looked like a younger version of Sting. He wore skinny jeans and a fitted shirt with wide, black and white horizontal stripes. He dressed like he could've been from Brooklyn, but he had an eastern European accent. "Is this your first time to Greece?"

"Yes. And you?"

"Yes, for me." He extended a hand. I shook it as he introduced himself. "I am Frederik. And this," he said, pointing to the shorter man who was too busy reaching into his black fanny pack to shake my hand, "is Zef. We are from Albania."

"But I have lived here in Greece for 20 years," Zef said. He pinched loose tobacco between his fingers and began rolling it into a paper.

"Yes," Frederik said, as Zef lit his cigarette. "He owns hotels and houses in Athens and Santorini. I am moving here to work for him."

Frederik's English was quite developed, though the lack of

contractions in his vocabulary made everything feel so formal. Zef didn't speak much English, but he was enthusiastic about trying.

At one point, an older woman walked past with her luggage, and we saw her struggling as she tried to carry it down the stairwell to the lower deck. Zef stopped mid-sentence, put his cigarette in his mouth, then ran to help her.

"Do not trust him!" Frederik yelled out to her, joking. "He is a thief!"

Zef was kind to old women, and Frederik was funny. That was the moment when I felt like I could relax talking to them.

Zef began giving me suggestions for where to eat and what to see in Santorini. He told me the best beaches and made suggestions for when to visit the museum. "Everyone ride ATV there. Everyone. But you do not rent ATV," he said. "I give you ATV." He pulled a keyring from another compartment in his fanny pack and pointed to two odd shaped keys. "ATV keys," he said. "One for you, one for Emily."

I had told them about Emily, but they hadn't met her yet. She was still in the dining room. "That's very generous of you," I said. "I will ask her about it."

"Where do you stay?" he asked.

I got a little nervous. "Um, some place we rented off AirBNB."

"I give you house. Not my house. Not with me. Your house. With pool. It is no problem for me." His speech was punctuated with emphatic hand gestures.

It didn't feel creepy, even though it probably should have. Still, I wanted to buy time before saying yes. "Well, we've already paid for it. I would have to ask Emily."

"It is okay," Frederik said. "I know this is crazy talking. Zef owns lots of rental houses for tourists. He wants to give you one to stay in for free. If you want."

"That's so nice of you!" I said, "And I don't know how to ask this, but ... are you ... going to murder me?" I laughed and put my hand to my throat, trying to step up my hand gesture game.

"No murder, no," Zef said, trying to assure me. He waved both of his arms across his body, the international symbol for "no."

Then Frederik, the funny one, took up where he left off. He made the "no" symbol while shaking his head and saying a long drawn out, "Nooooo," followed by a dramatic overhead stabbing motion, and said, "muuuurderrrr."

"Got it," I said, laughing. "Well now that you've promised not to kill me, which is obviously a binding agreement, I'll go ask Emily what she thinks. Be right back."

Four hours later, Emily and I stood at the back of Zef's car as he loaded our bags into it. Neither of us felt comfortable staying at his rental house, but we both agreed it would be fine to get a ride with them from the port to the city center.

"This is how people get taken," Emily whispered to me under her breath as Zef closed the trunk.

"I'm testing the locks before I even get in the car," I replied.

"I'm putting Liam Neeson on speed dial," she said.

"Good call. You can never be too safe," I said.

"Right," she said, laughing and rolling her eyes. "Safety is clearly the top priority of the evening."

We scrunched into the backseat, our knees pressing into the vinyl of the front seats. Zef drove and Frederik rode shotgun. According to my count, Zef had already rolled five cigarettes from the tobacco stash in his fanny pack, and the soot on the windows of his car testified that it was par for the course. Zef inhaled deeply as we took each hairpin turn.

"He keeps his Mercedes in Athens. You cannot keep nice cars on the island," Frederik explained. "The roads are too dangerous and narrow, and the saltwater rusts the paint."

I wasn't concerned about the quality of the car as much as the fact that Emily and I both get carsick.

"Could we roll the windows down?" I asked, hoping for cool, clean night air. It was after midnight when the ferry docked.

They both hand-cranked their windows open, and Frederik said something to Zef in Albanian. Then he turned to look at us and offer the translation, "I asked him why he never washes the car. How does he see to drive? The windows are filthy."

As he was finishing the last sentence, Zef motioned for him to grab the wheel, then Frederik steered from the passenger's seat as Zef climbed halfway out of the window and used his left arm to wipe the dirt off the windshield. All of this was happening as we rounded a curve. Meanwhile, Zef, who was still outside the car, puffed away on his cigarette and smiled at us through the windshield.

"We're going to die," Emily said.

"Definitely," I said.

"Definitely," Frederik said. Then as Zef climbed back in the car, Frederik said, "But only on accident. No murder! We promised!"

They showed us around downtown Fira and Oia, two of the main villages in Santorini, bought us lamb pita at a street kiosk, and then carried our bags to the lobby of our two-story white cave hotel at the northernmost tip of the island, making sure the manager was awake to let us in, then they waved goodbye to us.

"A murder-free adventure!" I said, eyes wide. "What a crazy night!" I pretended to wipe sweat from my brow.

"Hey, you prayed for free stuff," Emily said. "We just got free rides, free dinner, a free tour of two villages, plus free admission to the

Frederik Comedy Tour."

As we walked the wooden floors to our tiny, rustic room – decorated in all white, with two twin beds – we marveled that these men, who weren't Christ-followers, had been so kind to us without saying or doing anything that crossed into inappropriate territory.

"And He kept us safe," I said. We both slumped over to drop our bags onto the floor, heavy with exhaustion. "I also prayed for that." I opened the window to feel the breeze through the room. I flipped the switch to turn off the single exposed bulb hanging from a cord in the center of the room, and we climbed into our beds.

"I'm not sure whether that was a dangerous situation or not. But I'm grateful that God is our Shepherd," she said.

I am the Good Shepherd. The Good Shepherd lays down His life for the sheep. - John 10:11

In John 10, Jesus tells us He is the Good Shepherd. He protects and provides for His sheep. He cares about them. When they inevitably do foolish things or wind up in troubling situations, He is there to pick them up, throw them over His shoulders, and carry them out.

That's not to say troubling things won't happen or that we won't encounter struggle – just that His wrath falls to the wolves, not the sheep. Even trials are somehow an opportunity for Him to display His love for His sheep.

The Christian subculture has so many wrong ideas about how we get better, how we get clean. Someone tagged God's name in the lie, "God helps those who help themselves." Most of the time I can't help myself. Or I don't know I need help. Or I don't want help. I am a foolish sheep. In those risky places, the Good Shepherd reminds me just how good and strong and loving He is.

—

God continued to answer my prayers for the trip in nearly every country we went to. In Belgium, we caught a train to Amsterdam. A few minutes into the trip, we settled into a private hub with plush velvet seats and free wifi. A poised, high-heeled attendant came along to offer us free food and drinks. That's when we started to suspect maybe we were on the wrong train. We had not paid for first class, and this certainly seemed extravagant.

Twice, a man in a suit came through checking tickets. He checked the tickets of everyone around us, but walked past us both times, not even looking in our direction. When the train dropped us at the station, we discovered we were definitely not on the right train – the whole train was first class, high speed.

We were accidental hobos.

In retrospect, I wonder if God made us invisible. Or something. There's no reason we shouldn't have been kicked off the train or charged a hundred euros on the spot. I've heard stories of people being arrested if they didn't have the money.

But the Good Shepherd protected us from our ignorance.

Later that night, we were riding bikes in Amsterdam when the sky began to pour rain in sheets so thick we could barely see the path. Our clothes and purses were soaked through. The air was cold, and the wind coming off the water made it even worse. That's when we realized we were lost.

I was trying to stay hopeful, but then I heard Emily say to herself, "I hate this." A negative statement like that was unusual for Emily, so I went into problem-solving mode.

"Maybe there's someone I can ask for directions," I said. But there was no one in sight. Everyone had run for cover.

"As soon as we see a place where we can pull over, maybe you can take a look at the map," she offered.

I pulled the map out of my purse, which I had nested into the bicycle basket. The pages were stuck together, and the ink bled onto my hands.

"You know," I said, trying to speak over the volume of the rain, "any time I get lost for even like, 15 minutes, I get super bummed out for the Israelites."

She laughed. And to me, that felt like the problem was halfway solved. Then she saw a pub ahead and led the way as we pulled over to stand under the awning. The moment I opened the map, a red-headed guy stepped outside, shivered, and lit a cigarette.

"Are you lost? What are you looking for?" he asked.

I told him the address of our AirBNB house. "We've only been in town five hours. Can you help us?"

"You're very close. It's just three blocks that way," he said, pointing his cigarette over my shoulder.

"Thank you so much!"

"Wait. Wait right here," he said. Then he dropped his cigarette, stomped it out, and turned to go inside the bar. When he returned, he was slipping his right arm through the sleeve of his coat. "It's only three blocks, but they're three confusing blocks. I'll walk you there."

Emily and I stared wide-eyed at each other. This stranger walked six blocks roundtrip in the rain, without an umbrella, to help us find our lodging. When we got to the house, he just nodded, turned and waved, walking back to the bar.

The Good Shepherd safely led us home through the kindness of a stranger.

Later that night, while Emily used a hair dryer to salvage our passports, I wrote in my journal:

If I insist on living in my comfort zone, if I never follow Him to places where I come face to face with my complete inability to provide for myself or protect myself, then I never get to learn how good He is at taking care of me.

I know sometimes I live my life like a stupid sheep. It makes me grateful to have Him as my Shepherd. Other times, when I feel like He's calling me to something daunting, I can trust His track record of provision and protection.

> *Spirit lead me where my trust is without borders*
> *Let me walk upon the waters*
> *Wherever You would call me*
> *Take me deeper than my feet could ever wander*
> *And my faith will be made stronger*
> *In the presence of my Savior*
> *"Oceans" - Hillsong*

REFLECTION QUESTIONS:

1. What stories of God's protection have you personally experienced?

2. At times when we aren't spared trouble or tragedy, does that diminish the goodness of the Good Shepherd? What deeper truths might be learned in those places?

3. Is God calling you to something that may be considered risky? If so, what Scriptures or experiences reinforce your faith and help you trust Him to shepherd you?

17

WONDERFUL COUNSELOR

I bless the LORD who gives me counsel.
Psalm 16:7

I was terrified to visit England. For reasons I don't entirely understand, I struggle with British accents. They're lovely, beautiful to the ear, as long as I don't have to comprehend or respond. In the process of booking the tour, my management put me on a Skype call with the promoter but gave me no warning that she was British. I'm not sure why I didn't expect that. I spent half an hour on the phone with her, and by the end of it, I had no idea what I'd agreed to.

What I'd agreed to turned out to be an all-day women's conference. I led worship twice, spoke at both keynote sessions, then led a Q&A. The Q&A was the part that concerned me most – not because I feared I wouldn't have answers, but because I was afraid I wouldn't even be able to understand the questions.

Somehow, God translated for me. I came away understanding almost every word of English I heard, like I was living in the book of Acts or something. In fact, I was even able to relax and enjoy the Q&A session. In a moment of vulnerability, I shared my fear with the women and told them how grateful I was that I understood them all. They were gracious toward me, smiling and laughing at the ridiculousness of it all.

Several more questions came, and I felt like we were hitting a good stride. Then a lovely blonde girl in the back row raised her hand.

"Crayka scoufen slard bockta?" she asked.

My eyes widened. *Oh no, oh no, oh no …*

Then everyone laughed, and I knew she'd been joking.

"Oh thank God," I said. "Well played."

"I do have a real question though," she added. "I'm just wondering – well, you're single, and I'm assuming maybe you want to get married someday. Are there any Scriptures that have been helpful to you in the meantime?"

A passage immediately came to mind. I knew the verse and the reference right away. I started to share it with her, but then something strange happened. The verse I had in mind was Psalm 115:3, which says God does whatever He wants. For a fact-driven person like me, this truth is comforting. It means that whatever I've encountered is what is supposed to happen – singleness included. It means I can rest easy, knowing that God has done this. For most people, though, that truth comes across as harsh and emotionally unyielding.

The strange thing that happened was that I didn't quote that verse at all. In fact, when I started referencing the Scripture, what came out of my mouth was Psalm 145:17, and when I opened my Bible, it was the very page I opened to. My eyes fell right on the underlined passage, and I read it aloud to the women. It talks about how everything God does is His perfect kindness toward us.

"So," I said, continuing the sentence as though I had it planned in my head, "for me, right now, singleness is His greatest kindness to me. Marriage, at this moment, would be less kind, somehow. And if He brings me marriage in the future, then marriage will be the kindest thing in that moment."

God had delivered a softer message, shown a gentler side of His personality than the one I would've chosen to display. The character of God is important – the full character. But sometimes He especially reveals what we need to learn about Him in the moment, emphasizing certain shades intentionally. That lovely blonde girl must've needed His affection in that moment. While I didn't know that, He did.

I saw what You did for her, redirecting me like that, I said to Him in my head. *That was so sweet of You to give me different words to speak.*

I love watching Him love other people.

―

The next week, I spoke to a youth group in Madrid. A raven-haired girl with saucer eyes sat front and center, smiling up at me the whole time. The next night, I played a concert at the same church. The girl shuffled to the merchandise table afterward, with a blonde friend in tow.

The blonde girl took my hand and nodded toward the raven-haired girl. "Luz does not speak English, so I am going to translate for her."

"Great!" I said. "My Spanish is pretty limited."

Luz spoke a few words, her eyes filled with both passion and timidity, then her friend turned to me and said, "Luz does not go to this church. I invited her to come last night. She has been through many hard things and has been angry with God for many years."

I nodded. Luz spoke again, then the translator said, "Last night, while you were talking, Luz did not understand what you were saying."

If that was true, I wondered why Luz smiled at me throughout the talk.

"But," she continued, "Luz said it felt like you were telling her that

God loves her. She said she felt God's love for her last night, for the first time in her life."

My eyes filled with tears. I looked at Luz, and she was crying too. I leaned over to hug her. God is so big, so kind, to speak through me in ways that I can't speak. How great must His love for Luz be that He would speak so clearly to her through a language she can't understand. His pursuit of Luz was like watching a sunrise – you can see it coming, obvious and irresistible, pushing back the darkness.

I thought again of Anna, my hair stylist, and I smiled. What an honor to play a small role in the ways He dawns on people.

A few days later, I dropped Emily at the Frankfurt airport and flew to Stockholm. God had already answered the prayer that we would love each other more by the end of her time on the trip. I couldn't imagine continuing without her, not just because of the frustrations of solo travel – like having to take all your luggage with you when you go to the airport bathroom – but also because she really served as a reminder of how encouraging it is to have a teammate. I got to feel the fulfillment of making decisions based on someone else's joy, not just my own. Not only that, but I learned more about sacrifice and friendship from the way she treated me.

After she left, I kept looking for her strawberry blonde hair in airports, saving her seats on public transportation. It took me a while to remember that I was alone again.

In Sweden, I started every morning with a run by the Baltic Sea. On the first day's run, I passed myriad coffee shops and outdoor cafes. My former roommate, Swedish Lisa, who lived in her homeland again, suggested her favorite spot, a trendy shop with shared tables where empty seats were at a premium. But I felt a strange pull toward an empty cafe on the waterfront.

It wasn't hip like the place Lisa suggested, and the coffee wasn't spectacular, but I felt like I was supposed to be there. Every morning, I took my Bible and sat at an outdoor table, reading.

After a few days, the owner, a tall gray-haired man in his 50s, came outside and stood in the sunlight by my table. He wiped his thin hands on the legs of his black apron, and crumbs fell to the sidewalk.

"Is that a Bible?" he asked, pointing to my table.

"Yes it is," I said, beaming with delight.

"I became a Christian in 1977. In the military," he said. "Before that, I was an atheist."

We talked for several minutes before a customer came for espresso, so he ducked inside. After the customer left, he stepped back into the sunlight and said, "You know, I don't see many Christians. It makes me happy that you are here."

"I'm glad I'm here too," I said. "I'm always happy to meet Christians in other cultures."

"It is difficult to find a good church in Sweden. My wife and I haven't been to church in years."

I could not believe the opportunity God had put before me. I knew of two great churches in Stockholm, because I had played concerts at both of them.

"Well, what are you doing this Sunday?" I asked.

I recalled my prayer that God would bring me conversations about Him with strangers. In my head, I thanked Him for showing up at an empty waterfront cafe, walking off the pages I was reading, and entering into our conversation. He works out His plan in all things, at all times. Nothing is wasted. He even guides me to the places I drink my coffee.

I will instruct you and teach you in the way you should go; I will counsel you with my eye upon you. - Psalm 32:8

REFLECTION QUESTIONS:

1. In what areas of life do you most need God's counsel right now?

2. Have you ever felt the Spirit prompting you to do or say something unplanned? How did you respond?

3. Is it comforting or threatening to know that God is attentive to the details of your life and the encounters you have with others? What does His attention imply?

18

RESTORER

*I will restore to you the years
that the swarming locust has eaten,
the hopper, the destroyer, and the cutter,
My great army, which I sent among you.
Joel 2:25*

I saw it in a painting once and knew I had to go. The Duomo rising proud above the Arno River – though I didn't know the names of those things at the time – both lit up with street lamps and a sunset haze. The painting must have been thirty feet away from me, but through the thick street traffic of the art festival, I saw it and quickened my pace to get closer.

"Where is this?" I asked the artist.

"Florence, Italy," he replied, pausing to smile at the painting. Longing flooded his face.

"That's where I want to go," I said.

"Have you ever been to Italy?" he asked.

"No, but my work is taking me to Europe this summer, so I'm going to try to pull some strings."

By "pull some strings" I meant: I would try to book a concert there. And by the grace of God, I did.

I arrived in Italy to a stifling June heat wave and the highest temperatures of the year. The humidity and mosquitoes were inescapable. Saint John the Baptist Day, one of the city's biggest holidays, coincided with Italy's advancement to the semi-finals of the EuroCup. The awe of summer tourists, combined with the restless passion of the locals, made the city buzz.

There's an annual event called Calcio Storico which takes place on Saint John the Baptist Day. I'm fairly certain JTB himself wouldn't approve of it. It's a historic game of football-meets-rugby, mixed with heavy doses of ultimate fighting. Four teams meet in the street to vie for one ball. From what I understand, there are no rules. The locals refer to it as "murderball."

The match takes place in the piazza in front of a beautiful white basilica. The outdoor court is lined with twin-sized mattresses, strapped as padding around the perimeter. Portable metal stands surround the court, and a line of ambulances and medical personnel make up the outer ring.

I failed in my attempts to get a ticket, which meant I stood behind the ambulances. That's probably for the best, anyway. If you have any sense of mercy or gentleness within you, you can only watch through splayed fingers. I was grateful for a blocked view.

The event got off to a late start, due to some preliminary fighting on the parade route, which meant I only got to see parts of the first quarter. After that, I walked around the corner to lead worship for a church that meets on Sunday evenings. It was a small congregation made of people from 27 countries, all of whom share English as a common language.

Halfway through the service, a tall, broad shouldered man with a face like Heath Ledger entered and took a seat in the back. I stayed afterward to pray with some of the people in the congregation, but he must have stepped out quietly while our eyes were closed.

By the time I left the church, the Calcio Storico crowd had dispersed, and the streets were teeming with people trying to watch the EuroCup semifinals. When I travel, I always try to do what the locals do. The locals were footballing. Bars and restaurants all over town put out free hors d'oeuvres and drinks to draw in the patrons. A mass of people stood, stalled in the doorway, while others on the street leaned in through the open windows. Traffic couldn't even enter the one-lane roads, because the streets were thick with locals and tourists alike.

I didn't want a dimly lit bar, and I didn't want to be smashed into strangers. I walked street to street looking into the doors and windows, begging for an open seat at a restaurant or coffee shop. I wanted an ... *Oh! A seat! And who is that man?*

Perhaps I should be embarrassed to admit it, but I was drawn to him, even though all I could see was his back. He just looked so ... imposing. Goliath. Had he been a Calcio Storico player?

The seat beside him was the empty one. The only empty one.

When I sat down on the stool, the waitress behind the counter spoke to me in English, and I said, "I'll have an Americano, with one ice cube." The TV was to my left, but the sizeable man was over my right shoulder, so I never looked at his face or made eye contact.

I sipped my coffee. Watched the game. Within 20 minutes, it was halftime. I felt him leave. What a shame to never even see his face, I thought.

As the half wore on, the room cleared a bit. I decided to search the street for gelato before returning to my hostel to watch the rest of the match on the giant screen in the lobby, but I had no idea where to catch a cab. No cars could've moved down those streets – too many people.

I got a scoop of nocciolo and stood on the street, listening to the crowds, trying to figure out how I could get to my hostel. I leaned my back against the stone wall of the two-story building, eating my gelato with the flat plastic spoon in the brief moments before it melted.

Then I felt the presence of someone to my right. I looked over to see a man eating a calzone. It was the Heath Ledger-esque guy who disappeared from church earlier.

"Scusi, parla Inglese?" I said.

"Yes. I'm Australian," he replied, smiling.

"Oh, um … do you know where I could catch a taxi around here?"

"Sorry. I've only been in town for six hours. I came in to watch Calcio Storico." He wiped his mouth with a napkin and extended his hand, which was, if I recall, roughly the size of a three-ring binder. "I'm McClane."

He was a rugby player and had just flown in for the match, but failed to get tickets. Refusing to be deterred, he climbed construction scaffolding on the side of a building to watch from above. When that grew tiresome, he popped into the church to cool off and listen to what remained of the service.

After he finished his calzone, he said, "Do you want to go into that cafe over there and finish watching the game?" He pointed to the coffee shop where I'd been sitting minutes earlier.

We sat on the two empty barstools and the waitress approached. McClane said, "I'll have an espresso, and the lady will have an Americano with one ice cube."

I looked over at him, eyes wide.

He smiled.

"How did you …?" I asked.

"I saw you." He smiled again and slid money to the waitress. "I was sitting right in this spot."

Heath Ledger was Goliath was McClane? How was that even possible?

McClane and I talked politics and religion and music and art. He was an architect, but had lost respect for himself in the trade, and decided to go back into his family's construction business because he preferred to work with his hands.

We watched the game intermittently, talking and laughing. Suddenly, we heard noises outside the bar. Close, loud explosions.

"Let's go!" he said, urgent, eyes wide.

I wasn't sure what we would encounter outside. He must've seen the concern on my face.

"Those are the Saint John the Baptist fireworks!" he said.

I grabbed my bag and followed close behind him as he pushed through the mass of bodies to get to the bridge on the Arno River. For an hour, we stood watching. The show exceeded anything I'd seen stateside. I beamed.

The last lights and the lingering smoke faded from the sky, then we heard cheers in the street behind us. We ran to the closest open window to watch the last moments of the game, as Italy won and advanced to the EuroCup finals. The locals danced and sang; we laughed, living vicariously through their joy.

"It's too loud to talk here," he said. "Wanna just walk around the city?" We'd gone maybe a mile when we ran into two friends I made that afternoon – a couple who happened to be from the South Carolina town I lived in – and we talked with them for a few hours. Before I knew it, one of them mentioned that it was four o'clock in the morning.

McClane wrote his number on a napkin and hugged me goodbye. Then he put me in a cab to my hostel, and paid the cab driver. The whole night felt like I was living in a movie.

Many times, well meaning friends have told me that the reason I'm single is because I'm not a flirt. I need to "amp it up, turn it on, put out the vibe," they say. I just don't care to do that. I will give my affection to the right man at the right time, but not to anyone, and not too soon. And I've learned that when I think it's time, it's usually still too soon.

So I resisted the impulse to smile sideways at McClane when we met again for lunch. I guarded the angle of my chin. I stifled the wonder in my eyes. I'm not sure if it was wisdom or fear, but I held back.

We walked the cobblestone streets and happened upon a market that was going out of business. Everything was marked 70% off. For less than seven dollars, we got a baguette, prosciutto, fancy cheeses, a dark chocolate bar, and a liter of sparkling water. We sat in the piazza and watched as pigeons landed in swarms, then dispersed in every direction whenever a crowd of tourists walked through.

We tried to listen in on Italian conversations. He knew a little bit of the language, and with the lines I'd learned from the library CDs, we tried to translate. Our interpretations left us doubled over, laughing. From what we could tell, no one was going back for drinks at a hotel later – but that's all I knew for sure.

I knew I would never see McClane again, but the feeling wasn't weighty – it was helium, lifting and floating and waving goodbye over the horizon. For the first time since I met Joel, I had a crush on someone besides Joel. It was more than just the *I hope I like this guy* feeling of meeting Seabiscuit; it was *I like this guy*. What a gift of hope to know my heart still existed.

I danced barefoot in the fire once,
But only ashes remain as a memory.

I watched hope, like smoke,
Dissipate into thinning air,
And I could not let myself blink
Even for a moment,
Because the end the end the end.
My eyes memorized the way he evaporated.
I smelled the smoke in my hair
With every shivered breath.
And I believed through perpetual night
That death had come and taken me.
Even my dreams held only winter.
But then you, with your kind face,
Your strong hands,
And me with my heart full of echoes.
You rolled in with timber words
And you stacked yourself up against
My cold soul, my hopeless spirit
And you made me burn again.

I watched as God restored the parts of my heart that I worried were dead and gone. I love how He does that, breathing life into the places that feel like death.

Sometimes, when our hopes are decaying, He does what He did in Ezekiel's vision: he puts sinews and muscles and skin on them, not just so He can breathe life into them again, but so He can make them dance.

Restore our fortunes, O Lord,
like streams in the Negeb!
Those who sow in tears
shall reap with shouts of joy!
Psalm 126:4-5

REFLECTION QUESTIONS:

1. Have you ever given up on something only to see God do beautiful things to restore it later?

2. How do you know whether it's time to let a dream die or pray for His restoration?

3. If God works all things together for the good of His kids, does that mean God is involved in everything that happens?

19

PROVIDER

Look at the birds of the air: they neither sow nor reap nor gather into barns, and yet your heavenly Father feeds them. Are you not of more value than they?
Matthew 6:26

    The small, international church where I played in Florence relied mostly on tithes from college students, so they could only offer me a small stipend. After allotting most of my budget for gelato, I had enough left over for a hostel and a Vespa tour of the Tuscan countryside.

    After McClane flew off to meet up with friends in Scotland, I walked the cobblestone streets until my feet were blistered. Then I climbed three flights of stairs to my shared room in the hostel. The girls' dorm had 22 bunk beds in one room, no air conditioning or fans, and the windows didn't open. The summer heat wave cranked the night temperatures to well over 100 degrees. With the room's location adjacent to the showers, the humid air in the third floor dorm must've exceeded 120 degrees.

For two hours, I tried to sleep. I could tell that no one else was sleeping either, because throughout the night, I kept hearing curse words in various languages. I listened to some sermons on my iPod while I begged God to kill me. He refused.

When the top layer of my mattress was finally soaked through with sweat, I broke. Nearly in tears, I got up and lay face-down on the concrete floor, no pillow, no sheet. It was the coolest surface I could find. I fell asleep and woke 90 minutes later to my alarm. It was morning. I was still sweating.

—

The Vespa tour of Tuscany began at eight o'clock in the morning. When I met up with the tour group, I was several minutes late. Coffee in hand, purse slung diagonally across my body, hair in a topknot. I was a mess, but I didn't care. *"Just bring on the Vespas,"* I thought.

On the tour, I met a family of six from Indianapolis – parents in their 70s, their two grown sons, and their daughters-in-law. We rode together most of the day, sat together in the villa at the winery where we stopped for lunch, followed by gelato. Always gelato. As we sampled the flavors, I told them about the situation at my hostel and how I slept on the concrete floor.

Seven hours after meeting them, we parked our Vespas for the last time, then one daughter-in-law approached me and said, "I've talked about this with the family, and we want to invite you to stay in our hotel room tonight. It has air conditioning. We have a suite, so you would have your own section."

"Stop, stop, stop!" I said, beaming, "You had me at air conditioning!"

That evening I checked out of my hostel and rolled my luggage across the Ponte Vecchio to their hotel. I paused outside and took in the facade. I was staying in a building that was in the painting I'd seen at the art festival months earlier. The doorman let me up, and the couple helped me make myself at home. I threw open the curtains to find that the corner suite had a view of the Arno River on one side and the Duomo on the other. *"You have got to be kidding me,"* I prayed. *"Thank You, The Lord!"*

I thought of Philippians 4:19: *My God will supply every need of yours according to his riches in glory in Christ Jesus.*

It seems like a stretch to say a hotel room and air conditioning were an actual need, but given what the next few days held for me, maybe they were. Regardless, God our Provider stepped in to sustain me and lift me up. Since God owns everything, then everything comes from Him. Every good and perfect gift that comes our way has His name on the return address, even if it's delivered via the hands of strangers in a foreign land.

REFLECTION QUESTIONS:

1. Has God ever given you something unexpected and delightful? What did that reveal about His heart toward you?

2. In what practical way can you bless someone else who might need to be reminded that God is their provider?

3. How has God's provision for you in the past equipped you to trust Him in the future? What needs are you struggling to trust Him for today?

20

HEALER

Is anyone among you sick? Let him call for the elders of the church, and let them pray over him, anointing him with oil in the name of the Lord.
James 5:14

My short stay in Florence was followed by a week of U.S. Military ministry in rural Romania. My flight was delayed, and as I waited in the terminal while the hours passed, I grew increasingly achy and fevered and tired. It felt like the flu. I turned my suitcases on their sides and laid across the tops, then set my phone alarm for the time when my flight was eventually supposed to board. When I woke to the alarm, I could tell my health was going downhill quickly.

Hours later, we landed in Cluj, Romania. The head of the military ministry met me with a sign at the airport. He carried my luggage and packed it into the trunk of the Fiat before we began our two hour drive to the mission village, where military families were working to serve the poor.

When we arrived at the hotel, I was sweating through my clothes. I leaned my head against the wall and choked out a cry of exhaustion. An air conditioning unit hung over the door, one side lunging forward from the wall. I found the remote by the pillow on my twin cot, and pushed the power button. Nothing happened. I tried all the other buttons, to no avail. I climbed into bed and called the front desk to ask how to turn it on. The phone rang several times. No one answered.

I fell asleep with the AC remote in my hand, on top of the covers. I slept through the night, but woke on Sunday morning feeling even worse. I went to the hotel's meeting room, which served as our makeshift auditorium, to set up and soundcheck in preparation for the worship service that night.

"You don't look so good," Tim said. He was the man who booked me for the event. He had been with the military ministry group for a few years, but I had known him since he was a youth pastor in the States when he brought me in to play at his church.

"I feel terrible. I'm burning up. Is there a way we could get a box fan in here?"

He scratched his dark beard. "Let me call the guys. I think someone is going into town later. Maybe we can pick one up." We were so far removed from civilization that we couldn't take many trips to town.

"Thank you," I said. "That would be so helpful. Speaking of which, I can't figure out how to turn on the air conditioning in my room. I tried calling the front desk last night, but no one answered. Do you have any ideas?"

"Well, they only staff the front desk during the day. So that's probably why you couldn't get through. I'll see what I can do to get it working, but unfortunately most of the units in these rooms don't do anything. Mine doesn't work. It's kind of a cruel joke in this heat, eh?"

"No kidding. I feel like a spoiled American," I said, forcing a tired smile.

"No. It's valid. It's 105 degrees here. Plus, I think you might have a fever."

"I think I might have a coma," I said.

He laughed while furrowing his brow and pushing his lower lip out. "That is no good. No good."

—

That night I asked God to give me strength to lead worship and speak. I felt woozy, depleted of energy, swaying on the platform like a buoy in the ocean, but He pulled it off. At the end of the service, I went back to my hotel room and fell into the bed, where I stayed until the following night's worship service.

My room, which had a wall of windows, faced west. There were no curtains. I got the midday sun full-force, sapping me of all energy at the time of the day when I needed to be physically preparing to lead and speak. The next afternoon I woke to a knock on my door. One of the missionaries on staff had gone to town that day and picked up several rolls of aluminum foil so he could foil my windows to keep the heat down.

I hoped his stroke of genius would put me on the upswing, but I only got worse. My flu-like symptoms turned into a stiff neck and a terrible migraine. I rarely get headaches, so I tried to pass it off as muscle stiffness, thinking maybe I just needed a massage from sleeping on the hostel's concrete floor, followed by my sideways luggage during my flight delay.

The ministry staff had a meeting, without my knowledge, to discuss my downhill slide. A woman on staff came into my room on Wednesday morning. "One of the translators named Corina knows of a local doctor. His office is about 15 minutes away. She is going to take you to see him," she said. "This isn't up for debate. Get ready, and she'll be waiting outside the door."

Part of me wanted to shake it off, but I also knew I had been getting worse every day. I threw on some loose clothes and stepped outside to meet up with Corina, a petite blonde woman whose English was as good as mine. She drove me through the winding dirt roads of rural Romania. It looked like a landscape that I knew well – my hometown in the foothills of the Appalachian Mountains.

All I wanted was to go home. It was Independence Day, and I knew my family would be cooking out, watching the fireworks from the hill across from my parents' house. I thought of the military families we were there to serve alongside; they had surely suffered worse than this, in places they could not leave, for much longer than I had suffered. I thought of the life of sacrifice, how they yield the decisions about their lives and their family to an authority they may not even agree with.

The military kids probably lived in a deeper loneliness than I'd ever felt – always being uprooted, feeling displaced and unknown. I wanted to serve them, I wanted to worship with them. I could only do that if I got better. I asked God to heal me.

We pulled up to the doctor's office. Outside, a scraggly brown horse was tied to a wooden fence post, his mane in knots. I could only assume it was the doctor's transportation. When we walked in, there was no wait and no waiting room – just a metal folding chair outside the door. We knocked and the doctor came to greet us. They exchanged Romanian phrases.

Corina asked me questions on behalf of the doctor. He did various tests, some of them rudimentary, some more advanced. He pulled up a chair beside the table where I was lying, and spoke directly to me. Corina stood over his left shoulder, interpreting for him in the pauses between sentences.

"There is an outbreak of this sickness. You have meningitis," she said. "It is very serious, and it could get worse. He will schedule you for a spinal tap at the nearest hospital tomorrow morning. It is about two hours from here."

I racked my brain for information about meningitis and spinal taps. I knew that neither of those things were good. The thought of undergoing a spinal tap in a second-world country made me nervous. I grew even more nervous when he wrote me the prescription for pain medicine for the spinal tap, and it was 200mg of ibuprofen. I had taken 400mg for my headache that morning, so I couldn't imagine his recommended dosage would actually ward off the pain of a lumbar puncture.

Then she translated something that made me even more nervous. "There is swelling on your brain and spinal cord, so you cannot fly. You will not be able to go home for at least a week. Maybe two weeks." The doctor's eyes met Corina's, and they exchanged nervous glances. It felt like there was something they weren't telling me.

My flight home was scheduled for 36 hours later, when everyone else I knew was also leaving Romania to return to their military bases.

On the drive back to the hotel from the doctor's office, I began to imagine being hospitalized in a country where I knew no one and didn't speak the language. I watched in the side view mirror as a cloud of dust swelled behind us on the dirt road. Corina passed a man walking along the side. He was holding a rope with a cow tied to the other end. They both disappeared into the cloud.

She told me we were supposed to be back at the doctor's office at nine o'clock the following morning, so they could transport me to the hospital two hours away. I knew we would be driving the car to the hospital, but in my imagination, I would be transported in a wooden cart pulled by the doctor's horse.

Back in my room, I dropped into bed again. I pulled my laptop onto my stomach and searched for information on the type of meningitis they referenced. The survival rate wasn't good. Of those who survive it, there are often dramatic consequences – hearing loss, limb loss, vision loss, brain damage. That explained the subtle glances between Corina and the doctor.

The evening schedule included a service at six o'clock, followed by small group breakouts at seven o'clock, then an Independence Day celebration outside with fireworks and ice cream at eight o'clock.

The trip to the doctor stripped me of any energy I might've had for speaking and leading worship, but the ministry staff had already come up with a backup plan: Tim would speak from my notes, and a high school student would lead worship.

During the service, Tim announced that I was sick and asked everyone to keep me in their prayers. At the back of the room, the translators devised a plan.

Shortly after the small group breakout at seven o-clock, I woke to a knock on my door. The translators – Romanian, Czech, Hungarian – stood in the hallway. "We are here to pray for you," one of them said. "Is that okay?"

"Yes, please," I said.

A Romanian man pulled a straight-back chair from the table and pointed to it. "You sit here," he said.

"I may be contagious," I warned them. I sat.

They laid their hands on my sweat-drenched clothes and my clammy skin anyway.

Then, for the next twenty minutes, the translators prayed out loud for me, in three languages all at once. Chaotic and desperate and hopeful and beautiful. My shoulders shook. I wept. I couldn't move my neck or head, because of the pain and swelling, so I couldn't bury my face in my hands. The tears streamed down my face and pooled in the curve of my collar bone.

All my energy was depleted. If I'd had any left, I would've told them how much it meant to me that they rallied around me, talking to their Father about their sister. I would've said how beautiful it was that they cared for me so well when I barely had anything to give that week. I would've asked how I could pray for them in return. At the very least, I would've learned their names.

But I didn't. I just nodded and said a quiet, "Thank you," then they left me alone to sleep again.

Except I didn't sleep.

When I laid back down, I heard the door open again and I turned my head to see who it was.

Immediately I realized: I had turned my head.

I turned my head? I couldn't do that ten minutes ago because of the swelling around my brain stem. And I don't feel hot anymore either. And I feel kind of ... I feel fine, actually.

I was a little weak from not having eaten, but other than that, all my symptoms had disappeared. Immediately.

Tim stood at the door. He had come to let me know how the talk went and to check on me.

"I think ... I think God healed me," I said. "I'm not sure how else to explain what just happened."

"How do you feel?" he asked.

"Hungry," I said. "Like, when do they start serving the ice cream?"

He laughed, "Now that's what I like to hear!"

At eight o'clock, I celebrated Independence Day and God's healing with fireworks and a tiny cafeteria-style plastic bowl of vanilla ice cream and a flat, wooden spoon.

"For the record," I told Tim, "If I ever do go into a coma, just turn up the speakers and play Coldplay albums alternating with Matt Chandler sermons, and I'll probably come back."

"I'm not sure that's the best idea," he said. "You'd just be really happy in your coma."

"You're right. I didn't think that through. Play terrible music and heretical preachers."

—

The next morning when I went to the doctor's office, confusion registered on his face right away. Wide eyes, one eyebrow pointed toward his receding hairline. I felt incredible and enthusiastic about the healing, so I tried to make jokes with him via makeshift sign language. I pretended to choke myself, then folded my hands in prayer, made the "Jesus" sign in sign language, then smiled and gave two thumbs up. I don't think he understood, so I passed the conversation off to Corina for translation.

They exchanged a few sentences. He continued to look confused, gesturing toward me and my neck.

Then she said, "He says you are free to go. You do not need a spinal tap. And he says there is no charge."

"Wow! What did you tell him?" I asked.

"I told him that we prayed to God, and God healed you."

"Yes! That's what I was trying to say in my sign language! Dying ... pray ... Jesus ... happy!"

"I know!" she said, smiling and nodding. "You underestimate my talents as an interpreter!"

We laughed, and then I said, "Thank you for last night. I'm not sure whose idea that was, but I'm so grateful. I've never seen anything like that. I've read about it – I know He can do it, but so much of how I see Him work is through other means of grace, like medicine and doctors. I've never personally seen Him come direct until now."

"Neither of those ways are any less *Him*, but sometimes when you live in a place where there is a greater need, less availability of those medical things, you see Him move with greater power."

"It was worth getting sick to see Him show up like this. I'm thankful for this experience. This changes everything for me. This changes how I pray, how I hope, how I live." I smiled and hugged her. "Thank you for showing me more of who The Lord is, Corina."

Bless the Lord, O my soul, and forget not all His benefits, who forgives all your iniquity, who heals all your diseases, who redeems your life from the pit, who crowns you with steadfast love and mercy.... - Psalm 103:2-4

REFLECTION QUESTIONS:

1. What are some reasons we doubt the possibility that God might choose to heal in a specific situation? Are those valid reasons to question healings in general?

2. Have you ever experienced a miraculous healing?

3. In what ways might material blessings hinder our ability to tap into Kingdom things?

21

HUSBAND

For your Maker is your husband, the LORD of hosts is His name; and the Holy One of Israel is your Redeemer, the God of the whole earth He is called.
Isaiah 54:5

What opens your heart? I come alive when I feel smallest. I snuggle myself as close as I can to whatever reveals that light in me. The Moon. Orion. New York City. The sky. Dwight Howard's shoulders. Whatever. When I feel small I feel perfectly safe, because who would ever hurt something tiny? You protect delicate things. You are gentle with a fallen bird's nest. You don't put the wine glasses in the dishwasher. Jewelry gets its own box.

The way to expand the size of my heart is through the smallness of me in comparison to the largeness of something else. I think that's one reason why I'm so taken with The Lord. He is the biggest, most protective thing of all.

~

Pulling into NYC, I smiled at the familiar feeling of smallness. As Lauren and I walked through the East Village on our way to church, we passed my favorite corner, where park benches and pigeons and old Eastern European ladies converged.

Nostalgia swelled in my heart with every block we walked. If money were no object, I would buy an apartment on East 10th Street between 2nd and 3rd Avenues – just one block east of where I spent three of my favorite years – and live out my days ministering to the people of NYC. Despite the fact that most my friends got priced out of the City and moved to Brooklyn instead, my heart still feels at home there in lower Manhattan.

Lauren and I climbed the concrete steps and through the arched wooden doorway. The sanctuary lay before us – long and narrow, tall and dark, with a vaulted ceiling. The light of dusk barely seeped through the stained glass windows topped with carved adornments. We shuffled sideways into the middle pew on the left side.

"This is going to sound strange, but I'm glad you're here," I said.

"Yes. Well. Thank you for welcoming me to my own church," Lauren said, smiling.

"No, I mean – of all my church friends from when I lived here, very few of them even believe in God anymore. My friends who walked with Him and loved Him and talked about Him daily, hardly any of them seem to care anymore," I said.

I counted them in my head – the ones who still seemed to be walking with Christ. They numbered in the single digits.

As the service started, a man in jeans and a blazer took the stage to make announcements. I scanned the young, beautiful congregation and wondered: What had been the cause and effect of my friends walking away from Christ? Almost all of them, I realized, were drawn away by dating relationships outside the Church. My shoulders fell at the thought of it.

Afterward, Lauren and I walked to Peel's for dinner. We passed my former window in the East Village, and I tried to see if there was any tiny sliver of space between the curtains, so I could rabbit-hole my way back into my old life for just a moment.

Whenever that thought comes to mind, it doesn't take me long to realize I don't actually want to go back. New York? Yes. Old me? No. If I hadn't left NYC, I wonder if I would've followed the path of many of my friends and eventually left the church too?

The late summer night had me pulling my hands up into the long sleeves of my shirt. I shrugged my shoulders, let my hair fall down on the back of my neck for a little warmth as we took our seat at a cozy booth in the corner.

"Something warm in a mug," I told the waiter.

"Here, wrap up in this," Lauren said, handing me her cloth napkin.

"You think I won't," I said, tying it around my neck like a kerchief.

"Why didn't you bring a coat?" she asked. "You know New York in September: perfect days, chilly nights … "

Our waiter – mustached and suspendered – placed an earl grey latte in front of me and a glass of water in front of Lauren.

"My coat is currently on its way back from Sweden. I had to mail some stuff home."

"Speaking of Europe, any updates on Australia?" she asked.

"We need to have a talk about geography, Lauren. Europe is a contine –"

"Heath Ledger! That guy you met in Italy – whatever his name is. I can't remember!"

Our waiter came by to drop off our drinks and take our orders.

"We haven't looked at the menu yet," she said. "I'm so sorry."

"I know what I want, but I'll wait for her," I told him, waving off the menu.

While she scanned the paper menu, I scrolled through my phone. "Babies and dogs, babies and dogs. Wedding, wedding, babies and dogs," I said, mumbling.

"Facebook?" she asked, not even looking up from her menu.

"You know it."

She put the menu down and raised her head. Lauren looks like she's made of handcrafted porcelain. Her blue eyes aimed straight at me.

"You have my full attention now," she said. "Heath Ledger. Go."

"His name is McClane," I said, my cheeks blushing. I untied the kerchief and laid it beside her glass. I pulled my hair back into a ponytail again.

"Oh, getting flustered?" she asked, swirling the ice in her water.

"No, just – I haven't had a crush in a long time. It feels good," I said, smiling. I took a sip of my tea and paused before speaking again. "But then ... to have God do what He did for me in Romania ... well, that makes me love Him even more, too. It kind of puts things in perspective, you know? I love the idea of marriage, but I'm growing more aware of what it means that it's just a shadow, just a glimpse of our union with Christ. I don't want the shadow of the thing more than I want the thing itself." I set my teacup down.

"I'm with you," she said. "I'm starting to feel like my longings are finally in the right order."

The waiter returned, pulled a note pad from underneath the left strap of his suspenders, a pencil from behind his ear, and took our orders.

"I'm glad you're here," I said after he left, repeating my line from church. "I'm glad you're in this place in life, joyful in your singleness, walking with God."

I turned sideways, pulled my feet onto the bench and leaned against the stucco wall.

"When I was in Sweden," I continued, "My old roommate Lisa and I were talking about some of the modern misconceptions about what it's like to be single in the church these days. She said it's almost like there would be less shame attached to being a divorced person in the church than a single person in the church. Because then at least someone, at some point, wanted to marry you." I paused, thinking. "There are just so many layers of truth and lies and sadness in all of that."

Lauren nodded. "As beautiful as marriage is," she said, "And as much as I would love to have that happen, it kind of seems like that's all church culture is gearing us up for – as though we've lost sight of what is ultimate. You know? I don't want to waste this time aching over something He hasn't given me yet, and might never give."

Ultimately, I knew that marriage or singleness wasn't up to us. God's sovereignty over our situations was made evident in 1 Corinthians 7:7 when Paul talked about marriage and singleness in light of the Kingdom, *"Each has his own gift from God, one of one kind and one of another."* Both singleness and marriage are gifts from God – gifts of His choosing, given in His timing.

There was a heaviness in the air. We both felt it – that place where peace meets desire, where joy bends itself around longing. We looked down at our empty place-settings.

The waiter slid our plates in front of us at that moment, as if on cue.

REFLECTION QUESTIONS:

1. Are you content in the phase of life where God has you right now?

2. What good desires take your eyes off Christ?

3. What are some of the dangers of idolizing either marriage or

singleness, or even just the next stage of life?

4. In what ways could the Church work to reframe the view of singleness to align with Scripture's praise of that specific calling / gifting?

22
LIGHT

The Lord is my light and my salvation;
whom shall I fear?
The Lord is the stronghold of my life;
of whom shall I be afraid?
Psalm 27:1

Sometimes I think I could be really good at not getting what I want.

By the grace of God, I don't sin in relation to my singleness anymore. I spent years being tangled up in the standard sin patterns that bind many modern singles. Even within the church, we acknowledge that the purpose of marriage is holiness, but we act like the corresponding truth is that singleness is for hedonism. I know those chains well, and I remember their weight on my shoulders, the smell their rusting iron left on my skin.

I could point out the ways I've seen His Spirit developing His fruit in me over the past five years, but I could also point out some of the things I hope He will continue to work out of me in the next five years. I'm not there yet, but when the memories arise of who I used to be – bitter and defensive and abrasive – I'm grateful that I haven't gotten married a single day earlier than now. I'm learning to see the grace of God over every closed door.

This feeling of longing and anticipation is more universal than a desire for marriage, I know. Even married people or happily single people feel it. The longing is there, no matter who you are. It hides underneath the uncertainties of promotions and pregnancies, it tucks itself into the replayed memories of every failed interview and the pages of every unlived dream. The world is full of thwarted desires, buried deep, that keep rising to the surface. We all wait.

Sometimes trusting God's timing means we wait patiently, other times impatiently, but we wait. We refuse to build our own houses on our own foundations, because we know it would be laboring in vain, like Solomon said in Psalm 127:1, *"Unless The Lord builds the house, those who build it labor in vain."* We remind ourselves that Jesus knows waiting is hard. In John 13:27, as Jesus waited for Judas to betray Him, we see it. Jesus handed him the communion bread – the sign of His flesh that would be shredded and pierced in barely more than a dozen hours – and He told Judas, "Hurry."

I love being able to ask God to hurry, knowing He won't move a moment too soon or too late. It also helps me rest just to remember that He is in charge and that I don't have the power – or the wisdom, for that matter – to bring my own future to pass. It can be humbling and frustrating to leave it up to Him, but then I remember something my mentor told me once when I was eating Tex-Mex in Houston with him and his wife on a muggy Sunday afternoon. One sentence out of his mouth changed the way I wait.

"Don't light your own fire," Kemper said.

Kemper, with his white hair and broad smile, is a sage. If Gandalf were real and walked the earth, he would go to Kemper for advice. He is the Chuck Norris of wisdom.

"'Don't light your own fire' – what does that even mean?" I asked. Kemper doesn't usually speak in monosyllabic words. Half of the time I have to write down what he says so I can look it up later and not appear foolish. How embarrassing that I finally knew the actual words, but still didn't understand what he was trying to tell me.

Without hesitating, he quoted Isaiah 50:10-11 for me.

Who among you fears The Lord
and obeys the voice of his servant?
Let him who walks in darkness
and has no light
trust in the name of The Lord
and rely on his God.
Behold, all you who kindle a fire,
who equip yourselves with burning torches!
Walk by the light of your fire,
and by the torches that you have kindled!
This you have from my hand:
you shall lie down in torment.
- Isaiah 50:10-11

Isaiah talks about two kinds of people here. The first kind are the ones who fear The Lord. Those kind of people walk through dark times in faith, trusting that God is not only the God of the light but also the God in those dark nights. The second kind of person refuses to wait, impatiently grasping for matches or lighters or pieces of flint.

The second person, Isaiah says, may find comfort in their makeshift torches, but that is the only comfort they'll know. Their lack of faith in God's goodness, specifically His attention to their struggle, will torment them.

God doesn't just know my future. He built it. Scripture is always reminding me of this. Psalm 139 says He wrote our days before days existed. Revelation 13 talks about how the names of God's children were written in the Book of Life before the foundation of the earth.

He goes before me, He's already there, and He's in control. God's sovereignty is a prerequisite for the existence of prophecy. Otherwise, He would just be guessing. Somehow, He is not bound by time. He stands outside of time, already in my future. From that vantage point, He says my lot is secure.

But that's not even the best part. The best part is, even though He is outside of time, He is also, somehow, inside it. I do not wait alone. He is the Light that will be revealed, and He waits with me.

REFLECTION QUESTIONS:

1. Have you ever been tempted to light your own fire? What happened? What was the result?

2. When was a time you waited on God? What did that feel like? What helped you wait well?

3. What are some of the dangers of never having to wait for anything?

4. What lessons can only be learned through waiting?

23
FRIEND

No longer do I call you servants, for the servant does not know what his master is doing; but I have called you friends, for all that I have heard from My Father I have made known to you.
John 15:15

There is a point when you've traveled so much – when you've built a routine around daily suitcase editing, when you know how to put on exactly two pounds of clothes while standing in line at the airport in order for your luggage to accommodate the souvenirs you bought at the independent bookstore – that coming home becomes a burden. It seems easier to stay gone and never have to deal with all the changes that happened in your absence.

This is especially hard on relationships. Unless people stay in touch with you while you're gone, reconnecting can be clumsy and time consuming.

My housemates served me well in that – they were my people. When you're single, choosing your people wisely is especially important, because everybody needs Kingdom-driven teammates.

Prior to moving in with them, I spent much of my time in Greenville without a static group of friends. My friend group bent and shifted, people came and went, walked away, forgot me when I left town, grew into new phases of their lives.

Instead of feeling like an ingredient in the cake, mixed in and mingled with the others until we were inseparable, I felt like the oven. Because of D-Group, I had an obvious purpose in people's lives, and everyone expressed their gratitude for the service I provided, but I was always removed from the whole. The Spirit was the electricity – the power and heat and possibility. I was the conduit. But never the cake.

Most days it was easy to be grateful. There was beauty in it. But some days, when everyone seemed tucked into the pocket of their perfect friend group with their social calendar full of hashtag-BFFs, it felt like exile.

It can be a burden to crank out the heat, and some days I just wanted someone to let me be the weak one. I wanted someone I cared about to pursue my friendship instead of me always being the initiator. I wanted someone to come to my rescue, to show up at my door with surprises, to sit with me in the quiet instead of just the chaos, to fill in the spots on my calendar before I attempted it on my own.

Those feelings are selfish, I know. I'm not saying they're justified – just that they existed. But Butler Manor wiped them from the slate of my heart. God answered so many prayers through that house at 109 Butler Avenue.

Granted, the house itself was falling apart. There were roaches and mice, the winter heating bill was astronomical because the house had no insulation, a rotating cast of homeless men lived under a tarp in our backyard, and a vine had begun to grow up through Raicheal's floorboard. Once, Meghann came home to find that her ceiling had fallen in, along with all the water from the tub upstairs. And I was constantly waiting for the day the attic squirrels chewed through a wire and burned the whole place to the ground.

It's no wonder our rent was so cheap – no person in their right mind would've paid to live there. We didn't care. We celebrated it. The squirrels became our mascots, the homeless men our bodyguards. In that place, God displayed His heart for Kingdom friendship. He manifested His love through every prayer Meghann prayed over me, every word of wisdom Raicheal spoke into my life, every joke Jeannie told that left us falling over sideways on the couches. He was my friend through those friendships.

God made us to need The Body. I never want to feel self-sufficient, because that's a lie. I never want to push away from the table when things are hard or when I'm afraid of rejection. I want to remember the beauty of the Body of Christ, and I want to lean with all of my soul into the deep friendship that comes only through being a friend of God.

REFLECTION QUESTIONS:

1. Who are your people? Do they drive you toward the Kingdom and remind you of God's friendship to you? Or do they distract you from those realities?

2. What is the hardest part about living in gospel community?

3. What are the dangers of living outside of gospel community?

4. What are some blessings that can only come through living in gospel community?

24
SONG

The Lord is my strength and my song;
He has become my salvation.
Glad songs of salvation
are in the tents of the righteous:
"The right hand of The Lord does valiantly,
the right hand of The Lord exalts,
the right hand of The Lord does valiantly!"
Psalm 118:14-16

One Saturday when I was on the balcony reading my Bible and eating Greek yogurt with blueberries, I heard someone call my name. "Tara-Leigh! Tara-Leigh!" It was two people, actually. My friend Lee the pastor, and his wife Ali. They lived around the corner from Butler Manor and would take cute little hand-in-hand walks around the neighborhood on sunny days. The hand-holding was obvious because of the way her arm bent at a 90-degree angle to hold his.

She's a tiny thing, no bigger than a potted plant, and he is 6'4", all legs and shoulders. She practically had to reach up to hold his hand. He slouched to the left a bit, to make things easier on her.

"Hey, you guys! What a fun surprise!" I said. I put my Bible down and leaned over the edge of the balcony to talk to them.

"What are you doing tonight?" Lee yelled. "Wanna meet us for dinner at Stellar at six o'clock?"

"Count me in!"

—

I walked to Stellar, a tapas restaurant just a few blocks from my house. The nights were cooling so I put on black jeans, loose brown boots, a long tank, and a fitted caramel leather jacket.

When I arrived, they were already seated and had a glass of water waiting for me. I hugged them and pulled up the barstool. Ali sat between Lee and me, her long dark hair swirling around her jawline. She was smiling so big I could barely see the whites of her eyes.

"It's been too long since we've seen you," Lee said. "Tell us everything."

"Okay, I'll talk first, but then you guys have to take turns."

"Deal," Ali said, nodding.

I picked up my water and began to fill them in on the past few months.

Lee was the worship pastor at my South Carolina church, and we met through the music scene long before I ever left New York to be a part of his church. He knew most of my life stories, so I felt safe jumping in with the big stuff, no small talk.

I told them about Israel and how I ached for Jesus to come back, how I sometimes stand looking at the sky and pleading with Him, how He healed me in Romania, how I have a crush on a guy who lives halfway around the world.

At the first break in conversation, Lee said, "So when are you going to record another album?"

"I'm pretty happy right now, and I guess I don't write many songs when I'm happy. Most of my music comes from pain."

"So you haven't been writing at all lately? How long has it been since you've written?" Lee asked.

"No, not really," I said. "Well, I wrote a song last week, kind of a worship song, I guess." I paused, furrowed my brow. "And I did this thing a few months ago where I wrote a song every day for seven days, and I wanted them all to be worship songs too. So there's that."

"Let me get this straight," Lee said. "You 'haven't written much lately because you've been so happy,' but you've actually written eight worship songs?"

I laughed and nodded. "That sounds about right."

"Maybe, for you, worship is the art born of joy," he said, repositioning himself on the barstool. "Maybe God has been stirring a worship album up in you so naturally that you didn't even notice."

Ali nodded dramatically and laid a hand on my forearm. "Yes! You need to do a worship album! It's perfect!" She scrunched her nose, delighted.

I laughed. "How could I say no to enthusiasm like that?"

"But for real," Lee said, "This seems like the logical next step for you. If these songs are anything like the ones we've written together for the church, this will be your best album yet. Just let me know how I can help."

"Really? Okay then, I'll consider it. I'm excited to pray about this."

Lee's advice often hits me like Kemper's – they both know me well and have known me for so long that when they speak into my life, it almost always holds long-term value.

As I walked home that night, I thought about Lee's words: "*Maybe, for you, worship is the art born of joy."* I thought about all the times I'd had to praise Him in my pain. Sometimes it was work to remind my heart of the truth. Sometimes it was the sacrifice of praise.

Then I thought of how He had changed my heart into one that longed for His return even more in the beautiful moments than in the aching ones. I had hope that maybe I was starting to love Him for the fullness of who He was and what He was saving me *to*, instead of just for what He was saving me *from*. He had trained my heart to arc toward Him not just in moments of desperation but, all the more, in times of joy.

REFLECTION QUESTIONS:

1. Do you turn to God more in joy or in pain? Why? What does that reveal about your desires?

2. What are some joys in life that point you toward God?

3. If we really believe God is not just better than the bad things in life, but that He's also better than the best things and is, in fact, the Giver of all those good things, what are some practical ways to remind ourselves of that truth in the joyful times?

25

HOLY

*Holy, holy, holy is The Lord of hosts;
the whole earth is full of His glory!*
Isaiah 6:3

Curled up on the couch under the duvet I had pulled from my bed, I silenced my phone and tried to finish assembling my slides for an upcoming chapel service at a Christian university. My talk was built around identity and calling. In it, I referenced a few passages from the life of Abraham, but I could hardly bear to think about the things I planned to share. They were too powerful for me.

My hands trembled and my throat closed off when I first realized what was happening in Genesis 12-18.

In Genesis 18:1, an angel appears to Abraham as a human male, which is how they always appear when they speak to people on earth. Abraham calls this angel LORD. All caps. As in, YHWH, a name the ancient Jews wouldn't even put vowels into because they revered it too much to write or speak it. We translate it "Jehovah." In Genesis 18:25, Abraham refers to Him as the "Judge of all the earth." This is God the Father.

I knew about the Old Testament theophanies where Jesus, preincarnate, showed up on earth several times as "The Angel of The Lord." But the Father? The fact that the Father took on skin, or what appeared to be skin, stunned me. My mind can sort of make sense of Him as a burning bush or a pillar of fire or a pillar of cloud. But flesh? What a humble, generous God.

It softens me. It also terrifies me – in a good way.

—

When I was in Israel, our tour group attended a fascinating lecture at the Temple Institute. There, a group of Jewish scholars were restoring sacred vessels which they hope to use in the building of the third Temple.

They understand everything about Jewish history, but nothing about the new covenant Christ ushered in. They explained the priestly garments, blew a shofar, and displayed the exquisite detail of the golden menorah. They also talked about the veil separating the Holy Place from the Holy of Holies. In the ancient temple, before the Holy Spirit took up residence in believers, God's presence on earth was there, in the Holy of Holies.

The High Priest was only allowed into the Holy of Holies one day per year, and only then to make atonement for the sins of the people. He went through rigorous preparation before entering into the presence of God. There were bells sewn to the hem of his garment, so the people outside could hear him in motion. If the noise ceased, they assumed God had struck him dead. For that reason, the priest also had a rope tied around his ankle, so they could drag him out if he keeled over in the presence of God.

That information reinforces one significant point: the presence of

God is a bigger deal than most present day Christians realize. We have very little reverence for it. We misunderstand it, thinking we can "enter into it" when in fact, the Holy Spirit Himself has entered into us. We always have the blessing of His presence that many believers before Christ longed for and never experienced.

The word "holy" means "set apart." God is set apart. We are separated from Him. Yet He drew near.

"I led them with cords of kindness, with the bands of love, and I became to them as one who eases the yoke on their jaws, and I bent down to them and fed them." - Hosea 11:4

He bent down to feed us. He bent down to make our burden light. He did it in love and kindness. The HOLY HOLY HOLY God, drawing near to a sinful people. This is scandalous!

Do you want to know my favorite thing about the Temple Institute? It's the veil, the curtain separating the Holy Place from the Holy of Holies, where God dwelt. The veil was made of animal skin, sewn together, layer upon layer, to be two feet thick.

Jesus cried out again with a loud voice and yielded up His spirit. And behold, the curtain of the temple was torn in two, from top to bottom. And the earth shook, and the rocks were split. - Matthew 27:50-51

When Jesus died, that curtain, thicker than your mattress and box spring combined, split from heaven to earth, as our High Priest made atonement for our sins once and for all time.

As I stood in the Temple Institute looking at the curtain they've bound together for the Temple they plan to rebuild someday, I thought of how it's totally obsolete. I wanted to tell them about the incomprehensible beauty of it all – how His holiness, kept behind the curtain for so long, now lives within the bodies of His children. What does it even mean that a set apart God chose to make His way into my heart and never leave?

REFLECTION QUESTIONS:

1. What do you think it felt like to be a believer in the days before Christ came to earth as a man? Do you think it was easier or more difficult to love and obey God in that time? Why?

2. Can you think of any ways to be more mindful of the presence of a Holy God in your every moment? How would that change the way you live?

3. Is it comforting or terrifying that you can never leave the presence of God? Why?

26

RIGHTEOUS

I am The Lord who sanctifies you.
Leviticus 20:8

When Tom, the man I'd chosen to produce my new worship album, sent me the list of musicians he wanted to play on it – his "dream team" – I looked over the email on my phone, scrolling through the names. He wanted me to contact the guys to see if they were interested.

Then, at the bottom of the list, I saw it: Joel's name. Tom wanted Joel to play electric guitar.

I had written my previous album around the heartache of experiencing God's silence after losing Joel. The new album would have me praising God alongside my brother. By God's grace, we were finally at peace with each other – what a beautiful picture of redemption.

If a Holy God can draw near to sinful me, the gospel leaves no excuse for two sinners to hold a grudge. God has declared me righteous because of Christ, and every day He is perfecting that righteousness in me through sanctification. Sanctification is the process of God cleaning me up, transforming my desires, making me look more like His Son Jesus. It's a process He begins at the moment He saves us into His family, and completes on the day of our death or His return. Letting go of old wounds to embrace others who are in the Body of Christ is part of the sanctification process.

At times sanctification can be painful and feel like death. Other times it feels as easy as breathing. It is both. It is dying to self, and it is living to Christ. The fancy words for it are mortification and vivification – the putting to death and the coming to life. He really does make us new.

—

Recording an album is an exercise in learning how to make a lot of mistakes in front of the same people over and over. Fortunately, we'd hired musicians who showed grace and helped me laugh through the blunders.

When Tom was figuring out what tone he wanted from a song or a particular instrument, he liked to reference my synesthesia, a condition where the senses overlap involuntarily.

I have a mild version of audio-visual synesthesia, which means every sound has a color, texture, and shape, which I see in my head (but not with my eyes). I've been known to give bizarre descriptions of how I want something to sound. "I need the piano to sound like a barbed wire fence," for instance. Or, "my guitar is too purple. Can you make it more orange?"

After a few days, the band also started to play off this joke. One day Tom was talking through guitar parts with Joel.

Tom: "Can you make this guitar part sound like ... um ... the stars?"

Joel: "Sure. What key?"

Even visitors to the studio joined in the game. One day Raicheal stopped by and told me she thought a certain song should sound "like you're driving across Nebraska in a very ugly car."

We had a few running jokes. My favorite joke was called "This sounds like Coldplay." Tom and the band knew my weak spots, and they could sell me on anything they wanted if they told me it sounded like Coldplay.

Tom: "How do you feel about didgeridoos on this song, Tara-Leigh?"

Me: "No. Absolutely not."

Tom: "Oh, I guess you don't want it to sound like Coldplay then, huh?"

Me: "Coldplay has no didgeridoos!"

Joel: "Sure, not on their mainstream stuff. But on their underground stuff that only the real fans know about, it's basically just symphonies full of didgeridoos."

Tom: "So. Didgeridoos, yes?"

Me: "I hate you guys."

"How Irish do you want this song to be?" Tom asked one day, about two weeks into recording. "Like, I studied abroad there? Or I was raised there? Or I currently live in there in the mountains?" He swiveled around in his black leather desk chair to look at me as I sat on the couch.

I laughed, exhausted. "I'm too tired to even know what that means," I said. I coughed and took a sip of peppermint tea, coughed again, and set the mug on the round wooden table. I dropped my chin to my chest, shoulders slumping.

"Hey, I want you to go home," Tom said. "Don't come back here until you've slept at least eight hours. Maybe ten."

"But we still have the studio for the whole day," I said. It wasn't even ten o'clock in the morning yet.

"Don't worry about it. Some of the guys are coming in to work on parts. Plus, I've got a lot of detail work I can do here, editing and stuff like that. I just need you to rest before we start working on vocals."

I scrolled through my phone as I walked to the car. The booking agent I'd hired to book shows for my album release tour, who had been emailing me updates about all the wonderful possibilities lining up, finally emailed me to say he actually had nothing in place, and that he was quitting.

I backed out of my parking spot, and my thoughts erupted. Anger and worry and fear poured out. As I waited for a break in traffic so I could pull out of the studio parking lot and onto the road, I wrote replies to my booking agent in my head, wondering at how he could be so selfish.

Was he lying to me the whole time? Why would he just make things up? I wondered. *And now I'm too close to the album release to book any serious shows. I'll have to play a bunch of last-minute events for very little money, which means I'll be gone all summer and all my relationships will fall apart and ... I bet this guy has no idea the chain of consequence he just set in motion.*

I was furious.

The traffic opened up enough for me to exit the parking lot, and I prepared to floor it.

As I did, Joel pulled in, smiling as he waved at me.

It only took a moment for my thoughts to screech to a halt.

Seeing Joel reminded me: unforgiveness is too expensive. I spent three years hating him. It wrecked me. I gained nothing, and he lost nothing. As I looked back at his silver Mazda in my rearview mirror, I remembered how good it felt to be at peace with someone.

That's when I knew: whether the booking agent's actions were intentional, accidental, or just selfish, it didn't matter. I had to choose forgiveness. The state of my heart reveals itself in moments like that – when I'm tired and caught off guard and circumstances are frustrating. Those brief instances prove whether or not I'm yielding to His sanctifying work in me. But this lesson wasn't about the act of forgiveness; it was about the *speed* of forgiveness. Sometimes God lets us encounter the same struggles so we can see how differently we respond. It reveals how much He has grown us.

Part of sanctification is actually sinning less – growing in a desire for God while decreasing in a desire for the things of the world. But perhaps an even bigger part of it is the speed of my repentance. Growing in my love for God means faster repentance for even lesser offenses. This is where I can see the fruit of His Spirit being made manifest in my life. This is what it means to grow in His righteousness.

Tim Keller, my old pastor in NYC, says it's hard to see growth sometimes in the short term. The fruit of the Spirit is measured best over time. *Is it harder to upset me than it was two years ago? Am I more forgiving? Am I more patient with others?*

Discovering His righteousness in places where I used to see only my sin – it humbles and encourages me all at once. I'm humbled because I know me, so I know the good parts are truly Him. And I'm encouraged because there are still places in my life that I want to see less of me, places where I want to walk in victory over sin, to find freedom from the lies I keep believing.

When He lets me notice how much work He's already done, coupled with the promise that He will keep working, my heart is drawn to Him.

He never stops working, making practical righteousness from the positional righteousness He's already given us. He's turning us into what we already are, by His grace. What patient love.

Because of Him you are in Christ Jesus, who became to us wisdom from God, righteousness and sanctification and redemption, so that, as it is written, "Let the one who boasts, boast in the Lord." - 1 Corinthians 1:30-31

REFLECTION QUESTIONS:

1. When you look back at yourself two years ago, where do you see evidence of God's work in sanctifying you?

2. How quickly do you repent (turn away from sin)?

3. What area of your life is God currently pressing on in order to produce more of His righteousness in you?

27
STRENGTH

As each has received a gift, use it to serve one another, as good stewards of God's varied grace: whoever speaks, as one who speaks oracles of God; whoever serves, as one who serves by the strength that God supplies — in order that in everything God may be glorified through Jesus Christ.
1 Peter 4:10-11

One day while I was sitting in the vocal booth, I heard the guys talking in the control room. Loud, booming laughter. Deep voices. I just listened — not even to what they were saying, but to the sound of men. (If you're wondering what men sound like to my synesthesia brain, they are often brown and green, like a forest.)

I've forgotten what this feels like. I'm always around women. Sometimes it's hard to remember I'm different.

In the studio, men were opening doors, carrying my guitars, asking me if I needed anything. It was a far cry from the Alpha Female role I played in most of my relationships. I led D-Group in three cities on three different nights each week, which meant I was around 30 different women on those days. I lived with three women. I met with D-Group girls for coffee, hung out with them on the weekends, sat with them at church.

The joy I felt from being around the men in the studio had nothing to do with wanting a mate – in fact, many of them were married or had girlfriends. It had more to do with being reminded of how God made me different than them. He highlighted those differences when I was in the studio, and I began to ask Him to do that more often.

After I left the studio that night, I took my Bible, journal, and a fleece blanket to the balcony. Snow was in the forecast and I could feel it in the air. I stretched the blanket over the tips of my toes and began to write out some prayers and verses:

Will You raise up men around me? Strong men to show me what that looks like. Men who love You, so I can feel safe in that space. I just want to remember what it feels like when I don't have to take the reins or make the decisions. I like that kind of rest. It feels peaceful to me.

My flesh and my heart may fail, but God is the strength of my heart and my portion forever. - Psalm 73:26

She dresses herself with strength…. - Proverbs 31:17

All the strength I have is Yours. I want to be clothed in Your strength. But You also knew when to rest. Help me to follow Your lead: to know when to be strong and when to rest.

When I finished journaling, I walked back into the house from the balcony, and pressed the button on my phone to check for messages. There was one from Lauren Chandler.

LC and I met four years earlier. She lives in Dallas, and I stayed with her family anytime I toured through the area, but she and I also exchanged somewhat regular texts with prayer requests and life updates. For the past five years, she and a few other friends in the Dallas area had been trying to convince me to act on my long-standing desire to live in Texas.

"If there's a way we could work it out for you to live with us, would that entice you to move to Texas?"

I put my phone down on the square white table, looked down at it again, reading the text from a distance.

LC's husband Matt Chandler pastors a large church in the Dallas area, and I'd been podcasting him and quoting him at D-Group for years. He is one of the main tools God used in teaching me good doctrine and theology. Even more than that, the two of them together have imaged Christ to me in a way I'd never seen. They are students of each other, they love attentively, they repent to their kids when they sin against them, they disciple people not just to conform their behavior, but to press on their hearts. They make The Lord look glorious.

Immediately I felt like the answer to LC's question was "yes." But from the phrasing of her text, it sounded like this wasn't a sure thing on their end, so I didn't want to get my hopes up. Fear started to take root. Maybe it was a self-defense mechanism, but I began to think about how much I loved living at Butler Manor and how I could never leave it ... and within minutes, my head swirled everything around into a "no."

I needed to pray. Grabbing a jacket, I went back outside to journal more. The wind had blown the pages of my Bible, and I saw Psalm 81:10 staring back at me.

Open your mouth wide and I will fill it. - Psalm 81:10

Then I wrote:

Texas, Lord? The Chandlers? I can't imagine a better place to grow and learn and be sanctified and know You more and see marriage modeled well and grow D-Group all the more. Even writing this makes me want to sell everything and pack my bags. But please direct me clearly on this, the way You have with other big decisions in my life. Reveal the plan You want me to walk in, and I'll follow You.

It would require strength to uproot everything here and move there. But I trust that if You're leading me there, You'll be all the strength I need for the journey.

REFLECTION QUESTIONS:

1. In what ways do you try to walk in your own strength?

2. How can you begin to rely more on the strength of The Lord and the strength of others He places around you?

3. Do you struggle to rest? If so, what does that point to in your heart?

28

SOVEREIGN

We know that for those who love God all things work together for good, for those who are called according to His purpose.
Romans 8:28

Months had passed since I'd seen my family in Tennessee, so I decided to make the trip up as soon as I finished tracking vocals for the album. On a Wednesday afternoon, I drove from Greenville, South Carolina, where I lived, to Greeneville, Tennessee, where I was born and raised.

There are two main routes from Greenville to Greeneville. One route is more direct, over the Appalachian mountains on a winding two-lane highway. The other is mostly four-lanes and interstates, less treacherous, but it takes a little longer.

I opted for the scenery and curves of the mountain road. One thing I loved about that route was that my phone usually cut out. No calls, texts, buzzes, or beeps. I could roll the windows down and let the chill wash over me, listening to the river push past the rocks.

My parents' house hasn't changed much since I lived there – a brick ranch-style house on several acres of farmland. They're surrounded on all sides by family members or friends they've known for decades. When I come home to visit, Mom leaves me her spot in the garage. My dad and my brother Jon usually watch for me through the picture window, so they can come out and help me unload.

That afternoon when I arrived, Mom explained that Dad wasn't feeling well. "He was fixing something at the barn, and he pulled a muscle in his shoulder. Jon was working with him and said the pain was so bad he almost started throwing up."

"Oh no!" I said. "Where is he now?"

"He's asleep. I think he took some painkillers."

I caught up on everything that had been happening in east Tennessee, showed Mom some pictures from my recent travels, went to see my siblings and their families. That night I fell asleep in the guest room, happy to be home, but disappointed at having barely seen my dad. He was one of the main reasons I wanted to come for a visit.

The next morning, Dad was up before me.

"Poppy!" I said, hugging him, but trying not to squeeze too hard. "How are you feeling today?"

"A little better," he said. "My shoulder still hurts, but I'm not nauseated anymore. I could probably still win in a fight if one came my way." He took on a fighter stance and winked at me.

Over breakfast, he asked the usual questions: ministry, money, men. He loves the Gospel more than air and he wants to talk about it all the time. I always have something to learn from his experiences – the churches he planted, the evangelism he does, the new truths he has discovered in the Word. Lately we've been talking a lot about the differences in what we believe. They are minor, but still interesting to me.

"This came for you," he said, holding up the license plate renewal slip for my car. "Do you have time to go get it before you leave?"

"I was planning to drop in on Sonya at some point." My sister manages the bookstore our family owns, and I wanted to go see her before I left town. She was the only sibling I hadn't seen yet. "What time does the license place close?"

"I think they close at noon today," he said, flipping the paper over to read the hours listed on the back. "Yep. Noon."

I got up from the kitchen table, picked up our empty glasses and put them in the dishwasher. I leaned against the counter, facing him.

"If you want to go see Sonya, I'll go pick this up for you," he said. "But I'll need to leave now."

I smiled at his sweetness. He always wanted to help, even when he didn't feel good. "Really? That would be perfect! Thank you, Poppy! Then you and I can catch up more when I get back!" I hugged him, then poured the remains from the coffee pot into a travel mug, and headed to the bookstore.

Sonya emerged from the back office and grabbed me, "Hey, little sis!"

"Nice Harley," I said, pointing to her necklace. She and her husband own matching Harleys, and she had an assortment of Harley accessories as well. They're always going on some trip to a new Harley store or riding to conventions. She is the most mild-mannered Harley owner you've ever imagined.

After a few minutes of catching up, a customer approached the register to check out. I flipped through a book while I waited for Sonya to finish ringing her up.

"I've got to get these small group materials today," the woman said, "because I'm heading to the hospital this afternoon." I looked up to see her raking her hand through a large purse, black with decorative western buckles on the side. It was roughly the size of a beanbag chair.

Her hand emerged with a small black wallet. I wondered what could be taking up so much space in the rest of the purse.

She kept talking. Sonya kept responding. I kept flipping through the book as my mind drifted in and out of their conversation.

"Oh no! That's terrible!" Sonya said. Her tone caught my attention.

"Isn't it?" the customer replied. "I'm so glad we called the ambulance, otherwise we would've just thought it was his shoulder. But they said the shoulder pain combined with the vomiting let them know right away that it was a heart attack."

My eyes widened. I put the book down, moved in closer to listen.

"A massive coronary," she continued. "But the surgery went well, thank God." She slung the purse over her shoulder, said goodbye to my sister, then walked out.

"Did you hear that?" I said, incredulous.

"Which part?" Sonya asked.

"Shoulder pain? Vomiting? Massive coronary? I think Poppy had a heart attack!" I said.

"What?! I didn't know anything about vomiting," she said. "I only heard about the shoulder."

Of all the things my family does well, communication is at the bottom of the list. Perhaps I had misunderstood what Mom said? Or did Sonya just not have all the information? *"No,"* I recalled, *"Poppy definitely mentioned his nausea to me at breakfast."*

"He wasn't vomiting – just almost. I've got to go find him," I said, grabbing my phone and heading toward the door. "I love you."

She reached out to hug me. "Love you, too."

~

I sat on my parents' couch, anticipating my dad's return. I felt like a worried parent, waiting up for their child who stayed out past curfew.

I called his cell phone, but he didn't answer. Nervous and impatient, I started washing dishes, replying to emails, anything I could do to fill the time. Finally, he walked through the door.

"I have something really important to say to you," I said. "You aren't going to agree with me, but I need you to listen, please."

"Is this about John Calvin and Romans 9?" he asked, giving me a half smile.

"No, Poppy. It's about you. I think you had a heart attack yesterday. I think you need to go to the emergency room right now."

Last summer, one of dad's friends drove past a building my dad owns and witnessed two men, mid-thirties, breaking into it. He called Poppy to alert him there was a robbery in progress. Poppy called the cops and reported the license plate number his friend had given him, then drove to the building and pulled his truck in behind theirs, blocking their exit. As they ran, he chased them down and caught them. To me, he seems fearless.

He has lived through the military, a tornado, and probably far more close calls than he will ever tell me about. Despite the fact that he's relatively healthy, he doesn't like doctors or hospitals or pills or even medical opinions. So when I told him I wanted him to go to the emergency room, he turned me down.

"What about a doctor's appointment?" I asked. I grabbed the phone book, flipped through it, desperate for anything he would agree to. I pointed to the first name under Cardiologists. "What about this guy? I'm going to call them and see if they can get you in today, okay?"

I think he heard the tension in my voice. "Okay, but I'm going to be fine," he said.

The doctor's office couldn't get him in until the next morning. If he needed to see someone that day, he would have to go to the ER. He said no to that again, so I settled for an appointment the next day.

"I've got a field full of hay to put up, so this better not take up too much time," he said.

I shook my head, frustrated. "Poppy, the hay can wait."

A few hours later, I had to be back on the road to South Carolina. I hugged him for a long time. I didn't want to leave.

"Call me tomorrow after your appointment," I said. "I love you."

—

The next night, my sister Sonya called. "I don't want you to be alarmed, and there's no reason for you to come up here again, but Poppy has to have surgery to get some stints put in. He has three blockages – two of which are major."

Heart attack.

My first thought was one of ache – for him, for our family, for my deep longing to be with them in the midst of this.

My second thought was of God's great kindness. I think of how His sovereignty orchestrated the events leading up to this moment: my timing with finishing vocals in the studio led to my time driving to Tennessee on the day Poppy had the heart attack, which overlapped with the need for my license plate registration renewal which, had I not slept in, I would've had time to get on my own. But since I got up late, Poppy went to do it for me, so I could go see Sonya, so I could be at the bookstore at the very moment the woman spoke of her husband's heart attack, which had the same symptoms my dad experienced the day before.

I laid down on top of my sheets and wept in gratitude, tears spilling down both sides of my face and onto my hair and my pillow.

Through the tears, I sat up and walked downstairs. The light slid under Meghann's apartment door, into the foyer. I knocked softly on the white wooden door, decorated with a wreath she made out of orange fabric and burlap.

She opened the door and saw my red face, my swollen eyes. Then she did what she always does when anything feels like it's spiraling out of control, when anything hurts you or drops you to your knees.

"Can I pray for you?" she asked.

I nodded and sat, doubled over on her couch. She put her hand on my back and prayed out loud to the Father who calls my father His son, who loves him more than I ever could. She asked for healing, for comfort, and for redemption.

—

Two days later when Poppy called me from his hospital bed, he said, "Guess what. The nurse who has been assigned to me didn't know Jesus when I got here, but she knows Him now." I heard the smile in his voice.

"Poppy! That's incredible! I should've known you'd be the hospital evangelist!"

"Seems like this whole heart attack thing was a divine appointment," he said.

"'Divine appointment,' eh? So do you want to talk about John Calvin and Romans 9 now?" I asked.

He laughed. I beamed.

—

Your eyes saw my unformed substance; in Your book were written, every one of them, the days that were formed for me, when as yet there was none of them. - Psalm 139:16

According to Psalm 139:16, and many other Scriptures, God wrote those days in His book before any of them came to be. If God is sovereign – which is just a big word that means "over all" – then isn't everything a Divine appointment? And for those of us who know Him, that lifelong series of Divine appointments is for our good and His glory. We can take comfort in affliction, knowing His kindness falls on us even through the losses, the aches, the uncertainties.

Learning His sovereignty has brought me more comfort than almost any other aspect of His character. If you separate His sovereignty from His other characteristics like wisdom and kindness, it can seem terrifying and threatening. Because what if He used His power for evil?

But when viewed as a whole, the picture becomes clear: the God who is both infinitely good and infinitely wise can be trusted to do what is best with His infinite strength. Only He possesses those qualities to the full, so it's easy to recognize that I don't want anyone else in charge. I don't want to pin the less-desirable things in life on the Enemy – because if the Enemy is ultimately in charge of any event, I know he's not working for my good. But if I trust that every circumstance has been filtered through the sovereign hands of a loving, wise God, who ultimately uses every tactic of the Enemy as a means for His glory, then I know whatever lands on me is for my joy.

As for you, you meant evil against me, but God meant it for good.... - Genesis 50:20

He is nothing if not good and wise in His strength. His sovereignty, His over-all-ness, comforts me when nothing else can.

REFLECTION QUESTIONS:

1. How does God's sovereignty put the fears of His children to rest?

2. What fears do you need to release today? What unbelief do you need to put to death?

3. What Scriptures preach the gospel to you in moments when you're afraid?

29

KIND

I led them with cords of kindness,
with the bands of love,
and I became to them as one who eases the yoke on their jaws,
and I bent down to them and fed them.
Hosea 11:4

On an overcast, humid day, I walked down to the park and pulled out my journal to thank God for everything that transpired with my dad.

You are so faithful. I can't get over it. Thank You for Your faithfulness in –

Then I felt like He stopped me.

I put my pen down, stared at the pages of my journal, and waited. Something felt off, so I prayed and asked Him to talk to me about it. Then, like a clearing fog, things came into view, nuances and details of His character revealing themselves more fully.

I marked through what I had written at first and wrote:

You are so kind. I can't get over it. Thank You for Your kindness in saving my Poppy, in saving his nurse. Thank You for the stranger at the bookstore who may never know how You used her.

Then I wrote about the nuances I'd been pondering:

- Faithfulness is when You do something You promised.

- Kindness is when You do something You haven't promised, just because You want to.

You never promised we wouldn't have death or diseases or struggles – in fact, Your Word promises we can anticipate those things. You never promised to heal every earthly ailment, but You promised we could be eternally healed in the only way that really matters. So, in that, You have been faithful.

But in keeping Poppy alive through this heart attack, You have been kind. And the truth is, it would've been no less kind of You if You had chosen to take him. But thank You for choosing this particular kindness.

Recognizing God's kindness frees me up to talk to Him about everything happening in my heart. It banishes my shame and fear. It softens me.

I turned the page and kept writing:

I want to be honest with You about my concerns and my hopes and my desires. I'm not asking You to give me what I want or take the desires away. I know that's selfish. An immature faith asks You to either fulfill or remove my unmet desires. A mature faith asks You to purify me through any holy desires and sanctify me from any unholy desires. Purify me and sanctify me – I'm Yours.

I'm learning that vulnerability is a posture, not a reality. I may feel vulnerable, but there's actually nothing as certain as trusting You and walking in Your plan. To me, everything is uncertain. So I must be open to everything You bring, yielding, responsive. To You, everything is certain. You are forming the unshakeable, initiating, making.

Nothing is so restful and weightless as being vulnerable to You – where I am not my own, I am Yours, to bend beneath Your fingers.

REFLECTION QUESTIONS:

1. Describe a time when God displayed His kindness to you.

2. What prayers do you pray regarding your unmet desires? What does that reveal about your ultimate goal?

3. If you truly believed God's plan for you was the kindest plan, what would that change about the way you live and think and pray?

30

MAN OF SORROWS

*... A man of sorrows, and acquainted with grief ... Surely He has borne our
griefs and carried our sorrows...*
Isaiah 53:3-4

Shortly after midnight, I got a text from my sister Gina. A text that late at night was never good news. *It's about Poppy,* I thought, steeling myself for whatever information I was about to absorb.

But it was worse than I feared.

"Please pray for me. I've been having some mobility problems on my right side. Went to the doctor thinking I had a stroke. It wasn't a stroke. They found a brain tumor."

Gina, with her gentle spirit, her firm resolve, has raised three kids as a single mom. She has seen more tragedy and pain in her life than most people I know. My vision went blurry as I tried to fathom her having to endure this. I prayed, begged God to intervene. I had seen His grace and mercy when I had meningitis, when my dad had a heart attack – I prayed to see it again.

I sat in my living room with nothing to offer her but words spoken to Someone Else. I felt alone and far away when I thought of the hours and mountains that separated us.

"Praying already! Do you want me to come home? What do they know about it? How can I help?"

"I have an appointment with a neurosurgeon tomorrow morning. I'll know more then. No need to come home. I'll fill you in when I find out anything. God is in charge, and He is good. Love you."

"Love you too." I sat the phone down and began walking in circles in my living room, my shoes hitting the carpet and hardwood in rhythm. *Thud thud clack clack clack thud thud clack clack clack.*

Is it cancer, I wondered. Two years earlier, Matt Chandler had brain cancer, and I'd seen God do miraculous things to heal him. I wanted to call him and LC, but it felt too soon in the story and too late in the night.

—

The next morning, despite Gina's suggestion, I got in my car and drove to Tennessee. She was at her friend Cecil's house, so she gave me directions to come meet her there. Cecil was one of the instructors who worked at her business, and I later found out he'd taken over most of the workload for her for the past few days.

As I pulled into his gravel driveway, he exited through the side door and walked toward my car. He moved with purpose, signaling for me to roll my window down. Whatever he had to say, I could tell he didn't want to wait for me to stop the car and get out first.

"She's in the bathroom right now, so I just wanted to prepare you for what you're about to see. In the past week, she has lost all mobility on her right side. It started with her hand – she went to pick up a glass and her fingers wouldn't curl around the glass. Then it was her whole arm. Then it was her whole right side. She's walking with a cane."

My sister. Feisty, healthy, all spinach and kale and raw milk. She keeps bee hives and raises her own chickens. Walking with a cane? What was happening in her body? And how?

I got out of the car, shook my head back and forth in disbelief, and went inside to greet her. She leaned against a wall with her right side, cane tucked behind her, trying to hide the evidence, and reached out to hug me with her left arm. I wrapped her up in both of mine.

"I have some news," she said. "You might want to sit down." She shuffled to the computer desk and fell into the chair. "Cecil, will you pull it up?"

He leaned over the desk and double-clicked a file. An image came up on the screen.

When I saw the scan – an enormous blank white spot amidst the dark swirls – I knew.

"They can't say for sure without a biopsy," she said, "But it appears to be a really aggressive type of brain cancer. And if so, it's Stage 4."

I pressed my hand to my mouth. I couldn't blink, but I couldn't look at the screen either. I stared through the window and prayed in my thoughts: *"Jesus, You know what it's like to stare death in the face. Please draw near, shoulder this burden of grief and sorrow. Help me to press into You, to learn what it means so share in Your sufferings."*

For His sake I have suffered the loss of all things and count them as rubbish, in order that I may gain Christ... that I may know Him and the power of His resurrection, and may share His sufferings, becoming like Him in His death... - Philippians 3:8,10

REFLECTION QUESTIONS:

1. Do you believe God cares about your pain?

2. How can Christ's experience of pain, betrayal, and ache bring comfort to you in times of sorrow?

31
STABILITY

*I know, O Lord, that Your rules are righteous,
and that in faithfulness You have afflicted me.
Let Your steadfast love comfort me
according to Your promise to your servant.
Let Your mercy come to me, that I may live;
for Your law is my delight.*
Psalm 119:75-77

Every possible solution had a mountain of obstacles. Gina saw a handful of doctors, but no one would operate on her, and they wouldn't do a biopsy without a surgery. It was too far along, they said, hopeless. She didn't have health insurance either – did that play a role, I wondered?

I spent a day on the phone with clinics around the world, places in Mexico and Switzerland that used holistic and homeopathic approaches instead of traditional western treatments, but Gina didn't have a passport, and she was losing more mobility every day. "Decreased function means the tumor is growing – and quickly," one doctor said. "It's rare to see side effects increasing at this pace."

When problems arise, I shift into "fix it" mode. This, in itself, is often a problem. In the Myers-Briggs personality test, my type is called "The General." It's rich with potential flaws, but it's how God made me, so I tried to use that to serve Gina well. I researched, posted on Facebook, called friends who worked at hospitals. Friends and total strangers replied to me with suggestions on neurosurgeons. I reached out to every contact they sent my way.

I had to leave for a few days to lead a weekend women's conference on the west coast, but I kept researching and calling people. With each day that passed, the tumor grew. Soon, Gina wasn't able to walk anymore. She couldn't feed herself. She couldn't reply to my texts anymore, so I had to get all my information from other family members. Mom was sleeping in the room with her. It had only been two weeks. How did this happen so quickly?

I had seen Him save me, and I had seen Him save my dad, but I didn't believe He would save my sister. In fact, I was watching Him take my sister.

He has to take us all at some point, I know. The day will come when I will die, when my dad will die. So I knew the day would come for my sister too, I just didn't know it would be so soon. Even as my thoughts brought tears, I still knew God was good, regardless when He took her.

Gina knew that, too. "He can take me Home whenever He wants to," she had said. "I have everything I need. I just want my kids to be loved well and taken care of."

When all my fix-it strategies failed me and there was no longer anything I could do, that's when the emotions kicked in. After hours of research and emails in my Oregon bed-and-breakfast, I closed my laptop, climbed into bed, and pulled the wool Aztec print blanket over my head.

I was all kinds of sleepless, working my way into a deeper quiet than I'd ever known, as I carried the terrifying burden. Maybe it wasn't the truth, but it felt as though my sister's life was in my hands. If I couldn't come up with a solution, find someone to do something – and fast – she would die. I was helpless. I cried until sleep came.

The next morning, I went on a walk through the forest behind the lodge, praying and listening to sermons, so I could preach the gospel to my own heart in the midst of the struggle. A text message came from LC. Because of Matt's diagnosis, she had an extensive knowledge of brain cancer. I had sent her a picture of the scan to see if she had any suggestions. Her reply came:

"There's no easy way to say this. This tumor is very bad. It's in a tough place, and it's very big."

She was looking at the scan from two weeks earlier. I couldn't imagine how much bigger the tumor had become since then. As I was staring at the screen I noticed I had missed two calls earlier, so I checked the call log to see who it was. They were both from my sister Sonya. But I also noticed that it showed a phone call of more than an hour, with Sonya, earlier that morning, when I had been alone in my room.

I texted Sonya, "Did we talk on the phone this morning?"

"Yes. For a long time. You don't remember?"

I didn't.

I stopped in the middle of the forest, took my earbuds out, and looked for a place to sit down. A tree had fallen on the right side of the trail. I stepped over weeds and vines, and sat down, trying to piece things together in my head as I scrolled through my phone. There were text messages I didn't remember sending either.

My phone buzzed again. "How are you holding up?" LC asked.

"Honestly, I think I might be in shock. There are gaps in my memory. Is that crazy?"

"No, that does sound like shock. There are definitely physical symptoms like that. Do you need anything? Anything I can do?"

"Just prayer," I said. "I can't imagine how I'm going to speak and sing tonight if I can't hold a thought in my head."

"Praying. Already and still," she replied. Then she sent me the verse she clung to during Matt's brain cancer:

"He will be the stability of your times, abundance of salvation, wisdom, and knowledge." - Isaiah 33:6

I needed His stability. My footing and my balance were leaving me. I texted Sonya again, "Sorry I missed your two calls. Is this a good time to call you back?"

My phone rang right away. It was Sonya. I answered and stood to start walking again. I couldn't bear to be still.

"One of the doctors on your list, the one from Vanderbilt that your friend recommended ... well, it turns out Cecil knows a guy who knows him, and he's willing to take Gina on as a patient."

"What?!" My eyes grew wide, my mouth fell open in awe. I clasped my hand over eyes and steadied myself against a tree trunk.

"But just so you know – he can't get her in for another week. That's another week of tumor growth. And he said that this will mostly just be to relieve some of her pain and swelling to make her more comfortable. We can actually see her head swelling now. She has terrible headaches."

"When is the surgery?"

"October 2," she said.

"Byron's birthday," I said. Byron is Gina's oldest son. He had assumed one of the roles of provider for her since she got sick.

"Yes," Sonya said. "We're praying it will be his best birthday present ever. After the surgery, she'll probably go to rehab to learn to walk and talk and eat again." Neither of us said it, but we both knew those things were wishful thinking.

"I'll be there. I'll fly home tomorrow, then drive up."

Later that day, I got a text from Gina. It was the first time I'd heard from her in a week. It was only four words, but I rolled them around in my head, over and over: *"I love you, too."* I nearly ran my battery out, opening the text to look at it every few minutes. I couldn't imagine how long it took her to labor over typing the words with only one hand that she could barely move.

My final night in Oregon, I lay catatonic in my bed for an indeterminate amount of time. I couldn't hold a thought. I couldn't even cry. Journaling seemed like a good way to focus my energy, so I walked to the windows looking out at the forest, and I wrote:

Since I found out, I've tried to stay busy, to keep the thoughts at bay. But then I end up dreaming about it – her surgery, us waiting, the results. I'm hoping that I won't be filled with regret for the way this played out.

I wonder at her history – what was the catalyst that sent her hurtling toward this diagnosis, this creature devouring her from the inside, eating her movement and her words, turning her into a ghost? I want to rest my head on her shoulder. My throat seizes up as I write, remembering how I learned life from her.

Tuesday will tell if experiments and prayers will be tools in God's hands to pull her through on this side or to draw her to His arms. It doesn't even seem possible – either outcome – because surely this isn't happening.

―

On my way to the airport the next morning, my cab driver was playing Christian music. I don't remember what song it was, but I felt all my defenses dissolve and escape through the open window. Tears began forming behind my sunglasses. I worshipped from the cracked vinyl seats of a yellow cab.

"Excuse me," I said, my voice cracking. "Are you a Christian?"

"Yes," he said, "I came here from Indonesia because it is very hard to find a good Christian church there that teaches the Bible." I had a hard time understanding his accent over the *thump thump thump* of the segments on the highway, but he was kind enough to speak slowly.

We talked for most of the thirty minute drive to the airport. I had told everyone else not to ask me about Gina, and instead just to pray, because it hurt too much to talk about it. But for some reason, I decided to tell him, this stranger separated from me by a sliding plexiglass divider.

As I was handing him $40 for the ride, he said, "Can I pray for you and for Gina?"

I pressed my lips together, trembling. I nodded and leaned my head forward to rest it on the plexiglass divider. Tears fell onto the hem of my gray wool coat.

Then, with words I barely understood, my Indonesian brother prayed for the healing of the sister he'd never met.

—

After I left Oregon and made it back to South Carolina, I had one talk left to give before I drove to Tennessee. It was at a Christian college about half an hour from my house. Before I gave it, Meghann asked if she could pray for me. My housemates circled around me as tears fell on my stack of notes for the talk. My eyes were swollen and red. They ached.

We prayed, then Meghann leaned against her doorframe as I stood in the foyer. She crossed her arms and looked me in the eye, "Umm… I think."

She hesitated. Somehow I knew what she was going to say.

"I'm not supposed to speak from my notes, am I?" I asked.

"No, you're not," she said. "You need to talk about your sister."

I drove through the rain to stand on a stage in front of a chapel full of students, who fully expected me to speak on calling and identity, and I told them to scrap the slides, to forget the agenda. I picked up the microphone and sat on the edge of the stage and told them what I had been learning first-hand over the past few months, through meningitis and heart attacks and brain tumors: if we only draw near to God in struggle, it is His greatest kindness to increase our struggles.

REFLECTION QUESTIONS:

1. Describe a time when God was your stability. Did you recognize it at the time, or only in retrospect?

2. How do you respond when you realize God is giving a "no" answer to your prayers? Does it make you question His goodness?

3. How has God used pain and loss as a tool in your life?

4. Why is it difficult to value God over the other things we long for?

32
PEACE

Peace I leave with you; My peace I give to you. Not as the world gives do I give to you. Let not your hearts be troubled, neither let them be afraid.
John 14:27

Two nights before Gina's surgery, I woke from a dream, opened my laptop, pulled it onto my legs, and typed with my eyes closed. Then I shut the laptop and fell back asleep.

Hours later, when my alarm went off, my laptop still rested on top of my comforter. I opened it and typed in my password. The document stared back at me.

I will increase her years. Hers and her children. She will live and not die.

I vaguely remembered waking in the night, writing the draft. I wondered if it was God who had spoken to me in the night, or if it was only a dream. Would I choose to believe it was God's voice? Or just wait and see? Part of me wanted to post it on Facebook, an act of faith and resolve, then just let the chips fall where they may.

But I didn't. I waited. Mostly because I knew she was going to die. And since she knew Him, I had peace about the loss.

Gina had to be admitted to the ER early, the night before her surgery, because she was vomiting. We took turns visiting her in the room – my parents, her children, my brothers and sisters and cousins, Cecil, and even her pastor, who had driven eight hours round trip to be with us.

Her neurosurgeon was frustrated. Why hadn't we come sooner, he wanted to know. If she was throwing up, we needed to come right away! Why did we wait? The prognosis was already so poor, and now this? In the most crucial hours? How could we not have known, he wondered aloud. Our fears mounted in response to his tone and his questions.

Heaviness settled in. We didn't speak of it, but it lived behind our eyes in every moment. Every smile glazed over, each kind word weighed down. She couldn't speak or move – that had all been stolen from her days earlier. The doctors and nurses had begun to talk to her like she was a child, as though she couldn't understand. But I knew she was in there, even amidst the vacant stares and the mouth agape.

Around nine o'clock that night, they moved her to the ICU to prep for the morning's surgery. We were all allowed back to visit. The air filled with the sounds of dying – beeps and white noise and the *whoosh thud whoosh thud* of the respiratory machine.

I stood by her hospital bed and took her hand, careful not to press on the IV. "I think you can probably hear me, and you probably know exactly what's happening," I said, "But you just can't get your body to respond. If that's what's going on, can you look at me?"

Slowly, she did.

I almost collapsed with joy. I beamed. And the corners of her mouth lifted a little too, I'm sure of it.

The nurse, a quiet woman in cobalt scrubs and a brown ponytail, addressed her, and Gina's eyes followed her, to the other side of the bed, across from me.

That was a good sign, I knew. There was still brain activity.

The nurse said, "You can have one person stay with you tonight and sleep here in the room. Can you try to look at the person you want to stay here with you?"

I watched as her head moved ever so slightly back in my direction. She made eye contact with me. I wondered if she saw the tears pooling in my eyes. I wondered if she knew they were tears of joy and gratitude, as well as tears of ache.

I have said these things to you, that in Me you may have peace. In the world you will have tribulation. But take heart; I have overcome the world. - John 16:33

I didn't let myself sleep that night. I wanted to savor every last moment with her. So, as she slept, leaned over halfway on her left side, with her arm covered in wires and tape, and curled to her chest, I set my mind to memorize her. Mom had pulled her hair back so it wouldn't fall in her face. She wore a green hospital gown, the pattern made of tiny distressed circles, like a hundred glasses were left too long on the surface of a table, leaving their marks.

After I knew she was asleep, I put a hand on her shoulder, the other on her arm, and I prayed aloud. Throughout the night, I read Scripture to her, told her stories. I wanted to beg her, "When you get there, tell Him to come back soon." There. With Him. Where there are no more tears, no sting.

And I thought about Christ and His healings – how He always responded favorably to the plea, "If You will …," but how He balked at "If You can …." He always can. I know.

I thought about those words in that dream. I looked at my sister, her head swollen, face puffy. I was grateful for the chance to say such a prolonged goodbye. Most people are not afforded that grace. At least there was nothing left unsaid. To lose her would be to lose her into greater glory, into the arms of the Prince of Peace.

Yes, we are of good courage, and we would rather be away from the body and at home with The Lord. - 2 Corinthians 5:8

REFLECTION QUESTIONS:

1. How do other aspects of God's character – like His sovereignty and His kindness – help to set our hearts at peace?

2. Have you ever experienced His peace in what would otherwise be a crushing life situation?

3. Peace is part of the Fruit of the Spirit, which God grows in every believer. Since this is something that can grow and increase in you, what are some ways you can nurture that growth?

33
LIFE

...his days are determined,
and the number of his months is with You,
and You have appointed his limits that he cannot pass....
Job 14:5

The room was cold, so the nurse brought me a thin white blanket around two o'clock, when she came in to check all the levels on the machines monitoring Gina. At five o'clock, she came in with a team of nurses to wheel her into surgery. I stood up from the blue vinyl loveseat by the window, where I had been reading Scripture to her. I shook off my blanket to walk beside her bed as they rolled it out the door.

I held back tears, watching her until the roller bed disappeared into the elevator and the doors closed behind her. The last thing I said to her before they took her away was, *"Luh you too, bay."* It's how our family says goodbye.

Our family spent the morning traveling back and forth between her hospital room and the waiting room. Each of us was so tired, yet we couldn't sit still for long. I don't remember what we did or what we talked about – I only know what we thought about as we sat in the far corner of the waiting room, our eyes on the glass door where the doctor would appear whenever he finished the surgery. They said it would take seven hours.

The quiet cold of the waiting room preserved all our fears. We were frozen in the stillness. Occasionally we shuffled to another part of the room, wrapped in blankets, to talk with the other families. We shared stories. Some of them had makeshift homes set up there: heirloom quilts and airline pillows and rolling coolers, plastic storage bins full of pre-packaged foods, paper plates, plastic cutlery. They kept their toothbrushes and shower gels in overnight bags. They had known this struggle far longer than we had.

Around the fifth hour of surgery, he appeared. My dad went to him first. We stood a few feet away, eavesdropping, as though the buffer of space and volume would soften the blow.

"I don't know how to say this," the doctor began, "but I think we got it all."

Excuse me?

"It looked like ... like the cancer had grown back into itself somehow. Cancer doesn't really do that, so we're not sure what happened, except to say ... it was like ... like someone had been in there before me."

Someone. Indeed.

"Every MRI showed it as unencapsulated," he said, his eyes and his smile both wide, "but ... I just ... scooped it out."

For by Him all things were created, in heaven and on earth, visible and invisible, whether thrones or dominions or rulers or authorities – all things were created through Him and for Him. And He is before all things, and in Him all things hold together. - Colossians 1:16-17

I remembered my dream and wondered again, *"Was that You?"*

The post-op MRI came back, showing that the doctor had gotten all of the tumor, just as he thought. Gina became the talk of the Critical Care Unit. Other doctors and nurses came by to see the miracle that had transpired.

"I don't want to be the focus of all this," she said – *because she could talk again* – "I want *God* to be. He did this. Not me."

When the therapist came to the room to introduce herself and assess Gina's state of need, Gina was feeding herself. "I've heard you're doing really well, and I just wanted to see for myself," the therapist said.

"Thank you so much!" Gina said, smiling. Then she tilted her head and said, "I mean this in the nicest way possible – we don't need you."

We all laughed. Some of us wept.

The therapist wrapped an arm around Gina and smiled. "I'm glad to see you are absolutely right."

Gina walked to her wheelchair the next day. Then, even though the doctors said she'd need to stay in CCU for a week and then go to a rehab facility for months afterward, they sent her home 48 hours after her brain surgery.

~

The most obvious things to feel at times of healing are things like joy and gratitude and awe. But no one ever tells you about the humility. I was overwhelmed with how humbling this healing was.

Do you know why this absolutely laid me on my face? Because I didn't believe. I knew she was going to die – either in the surgery or shortly after, from the cancer. I did not muster up some big amount of faith and offer it to Him so that He could respond to it with measured amounts of grace, perfectly suited to the size of my faith.

No. His goodness doesn't rest on my faith. It rests on His character, despite my faithlessness. What He did was far more generous and kind than my filthy-rags faith could ever merit.

It reminds me of all the ways He heals and saves. My salvation had nothing to do with me – I didn't even provide the faith for it! The only thing I brought to the table was my sin. And He traded it for Life.

REFLECTION QUESTIONS:

1. What are some of the dangers of trying to use our faith as a bargaining chip to get what we want from God?

2. What makes the distinction between regular life and the "abundant life" that Jesus came to bring His followers (John 10:10)? Is it possible for poor, sick, hurting people to have abundant life?

3. Is any sort of striving or entitlement holding you back from walking in the fullness of life God has for you?

34
GUIDE

This is God, our God forever and ever.
He will guide us forever.
Psalm 48:14

Halfway across the mountains of North Carolina, I slowed and pulled my car into a tiny gravel parking spot wedged up against the pine trees. I was on my way to lead worship at a church in Charlotte, and I had some time to spare.

The soundtrack of the river created a serene place in my mind to talk to God. I wanted to talk about Texas. The thought of moving there hadn't left the back of my mind since LC first mentioned it to me months earlier.

I pulled out my journal and climbed onto the hood of my car.

I feel like Texas might be where You're leading me, but the timing never seems to align, and then I start to doubt. I know You have a plan – You wrote it long before the foundation of the world. You pave highways with your words. Flatten mountains, unearth pines. Once, your words met with water, and the result was the Sahara Desert – right through the Red Sea. So do what You will. Make Your plan clear. I take comfort in this:

The Lord will fulfill all His purpose for me. - Psalm 138:8

The Lord.
Will.
Fulfill.
The Lord will fulfill.
All.
His purpose.
The Lord will fulfill all His purpose.
His purpose for me.
The Lord will fulfill all His purpose for me.

This passage from Your Word is so comforting to me. It's the most rest-inducing truth. You hold it all, do it all. I don't have to struggle or worry. Whatever Your plan for me, I know You're going to work it out through me. When I remember the truth of the situation – that my life is just a secret I have to hear and not a decision I have to make – I feel Your peace wrap around me. Thank You.

I closed my journal and ducked back into the car for the rest of the drive.

———

While waiting for my soundcheck before the conference, I decided to catch up on email at a coffee shop. The barista called "TLC!" over my shoulder, and I walked to the counter to pick up the flat white, my favorite underrated coffee drink. A few sips into the drink, a new email showed up in my inbox. It was from LC.

"It's official: the Chandlers would like to welcome you into our home! It's nothing fancy, but we're happy to have you join us! Does June work?"

I replied to LC and said, "Seriously? Hooray! Count me in!" I smiled, shook my head. Texas had been a prayer for nearly a decade, and it was finally happening. In fact, Texas was an answer to many prayers, most of which seemed unrelated, and some of which it felt like God had been ignoring for years. But in one fell swoop, He gave a "yes" to several separate prayers. I never imagined they would all be resolved with one answer. He's so efficient.

A picture of His "yes" began to emerge, one pixel at a time:

1. Sanctification: Living at Butler Manor had been a dream, but it was almost too easy. I complained to Raicheal and Meghann and Jeannie, saying they were so ideal as housemates that it wasn't even sanctifying.

When you live with peers, and you all are maturing in your relationships with Christ, the bumps in the road are fewer and further between. I loved that feeling of coasting, but I also knew there was more for me to learn, especially if God had marriage as part of His plan for me.

With peers, you can negotiate. *"Since you like it cooler than I do in the summer, could we keep the temperature where you want it, but then you also pay a little more toward the electric bill?"*

In someone else's home, however, you just have to yield. I wouldn't get to decide the temperature, the decor wouldn't be up to me, and my vote wouldn't count if they suddenly decided, for instance, to turn their home into a feral cat shelter. I wanted to learn what it was like to submit, not just compromise.

2. Nurturing: I had been praying that God would help me be more nurturing. Most of my life is spent interacting with people I can reason with. *"I'd love to chat, but I'm late for a meeting. Can I call you back?"* The Chandlers have three children, and everyone knows you can't reason with a child.

I told Matt and LC, "I've never lived with kids. I'm the youngest in my family, and I never babysat. So I need you to know up front that

I'm terrified of your four year old. I don't know what to talk to her about, and I'm afraid she'll hate me. But I want to learn."

They laughed and promised me that Norah was a piece of cake. But I was still nervous, planning questions in advance of my arrival, practicing my silly faces, and brushing up on jump rope skills. I had no idea what to expect, but I knew this was a chance for me to grow and probably to fall in love with the three kids in the family.

3. Diversity: My life in South Carolina had me spending most of my time around females. I'd asked God to put me around godly men, so I could see what that looked like – in marriage, in leadership, in everyday life. I didn't want to be the alpha in every situation. I could think of no better scenario for learning that lesson than in the home of one of the men I respected most.

4. Authority: By that point, D-Group had grown to more than 20 groups around the country. As a single female in full-time ministry, not on staff at a church, and in leadership over such a large number of people, I needed authority in my life – tangible, present authority. To lead well, I needed to follow well. What better way to maximize the Gospel than to live with and be discipled by those who know Him better?

~

In the midst of a chapter about humility and pouring ourselves out to others, God gives a beautiful picture of how He guides us:

The Lord will guide you continually and satisfy your desire in scorched places and make your bones strong; and you shall be like a watered garden, like a spring of water, whose waters do not fail. And your ancient ruins shall be rebuilt; you shall raise up the foundations of many generations; you shall be called the repairer of the breach, the restorer of streets to dwell in. - Isaiah 58:11-12

I believe in a sovereign God who orchestrates His plans for us, who hears our cries for guidance and answers us through His Word as well as through circumstances, peace, and the wisdom of others.

Sometimes following His guidance means we get to take hold of things we've always prayed for, and sometimes it means laying down something beautiful to be guided into a desert, and sometimes it means both of those things at once.

Nothing in me wanted to leave South Carolina. I adored it. But trusting God and His plan for my good and His glory, I packed my bags. It was time to say goodbye to the rolling hills and travel to the scorched places. I prayed He would make me into a spring.

REFLECTION QUESTIONS:

1. Do you believe God has a plan for your life? Or is it mostly up to you to map things out?

2. If God has a plan, what are some ways you can set your heart to discern it? Is anything currently distracting you from seeking His guidance in that?

3. What fears do you have about yielding your life to God's guidance and purposes? What aspects of God's characters might help settle those fears?

35
GIVER

*Every good gift and every perfect gift is from above,
coming down from the Father of lights....*
James 1:17

Most single women have this want. It's huge. It feels like a suitcase filled with Someday, and you have to carry it around until you find a place to leave it. You can hardly ever forget it's there, because it tears at the skin on your hands, and it makes your back ache, and it slows you down at the crosswalk.

But God is smart and efficient. Everything He packed into the suitcase has a rightful place.

Something in me comes alive when I can serve someone with my own hands – food and drink and cleaning and comforts. I *float* when I get to do this. So is God cruel that I don't have a husband? No, on the contrary – He revealed that I could do almost all those things for my housemates and D-Group and for the homeless men and women who gathered around Butler Manor. It's like God is saying, *"Here's* where to put that desire."

I love deep conversation. I want this in a Someday. But even though Someday isn't here, God hasn't robbed me of that. I have it in my accountability partner, in the women who walk alongside me in D-Group. I am known, loved. It feels like God is saying, *"This* desire fits *here."*

Sanctification is one of the most beautiful aspects of Someday, I'm certain. But He feeds me from His hand already. He teaches me, puts people around me to slough off the rough edges and bear with me as I learn. It's as though He's saying, "Yes, I gave you this desire. So let me meet it – even if it's in a way you don't expect."

The only deep desire I have that can't be fulfilled outside of marriage is such a shadow, *a flat, black, two-dimensional, passing image of what unity with Him is like, anyway.* And even that desire gets me more of Christ – more patience, more holiness, more dying to self.

How absolutely brilliant of God to give me all these things in the present. I'm not waiting for my desires to be fulfilled. They are. And no, surely it's not the same, but I don't want to miss this. This present singleness is from Him. So I repeat it to myself sometimes when I'm tempted to lean too much toward Someday: Everything I have is from God. Everything I do not have is also from God. And both of those truths are good.

Yes, the LORD will give what is good, and our land will yield its increase. – Psalm 85:12

REFLECTION QUESTIONS:

1. Do you believe God gives good gifts?

2. If you feel like God is holding out on you, what does that reveal about what you think of His character? What does it reveal about your heart?

3. Do you trust God to actually give you new and better desires in your heart?

36

KEEPER

The Lord is your keeper;
The Lord is your shade on your right hand ...
The Lord will keep
your going out and your coming in
from this time forth and forevermore.
Psalm 121:5, 8

I got the call from the cardiologist. The results were in from my last echocardiogram and EKG, and he wanted to see me.

I climbed onto the crunchy white paper pulled taut against the hospital blue vinyl of the exam table. The room was cold. I wanted to do jumping jacks to warm up, but at any minute, the doctor was going to walk in and listen to my heart, and I didn't want it to be racing. Instead, I picked up the eight month old copy of *Vogue* and started reading an article about Salvatore Ferragamo's childhood.

My heart sounds like a broken washing machine, from what the doctors say. I'm sure there's some kind of spiritual lesson in that. All I was thinking about though, were the test results. Someday, they say, I'll have to have open heart surgery, but they've always said it's likely a long way off. My annual tests just serve to keep me in check.

My new doctor walked in, chart in hand, stethoscope around his neck, and greeted me with a firm nod. He was not a warm man. It felt like the temperature in the room actually dropped when he entered. He was very serious, his brow permanently furrowed. His eyes were dark and ominous. He cleared his throat a lot. Basically, he was like the villain in any comic book, minus the evil laugh, because he showed no emotion.

"What have you been doing?" he asked.

"Just flipping through this magazine," I said, holding up the *Vogue*.

"No. What have you been doing that would make your aorta increase in size so much? I see that you don't smoke. But have you been lifting weights? Drinking lots of caffeine? Excessive cardio?"

"Um ... Check. Check. Check."

He listened to my heart and wrote some numbers on his chart.

"Your heart problem has not gotten worse in all the years doctors have been monitoring it. But things are progressing now, so I need to see you every six months."

I nodded.

"And here are the new rules –" he said, ticking each rule off with his fingers in the air, "No lifting anything more than 20 pounds, no more than one cup of coffee per day, and no excessive cardio."

"But I'm a distance runner. Is that okay?"

"I need your heart rate to stay in this range," he said, pointing to a chart on the wall. "If you can run and keep it in that range, fine. But most distance runners range much higher than that. Do you understand?"

"Yes."

"Listen. The decision about when you have this surgery – it is not up to you, it is up to me."

"I understand. Thank you." I nodded, pursing my lips to ward off the tears.

"I am writing you a prescription," he said, "You will need to take this every day for the rest of your life."

"Okay," I said. I didn't question him. He caught me off guard.

I paid my bill, and walked through the smoke-stained lobby – no one is allowed to smoke in there, but almost every cardiology patient smokes, so the room always carries the stench of old cigarettes. I pushed the glass door open and walked past a man inhaling the stubby remains of his Marlboro before nodding at me and crushing it under his toe. I climbed into my car and stared at the windshield – not through it, at it.

God healed my meningitis. God healed my sister's cancer. Does He always heal everything? If so, how do people ever get to die and go be with Him? Should I expect Him to heal my congenital heart defects? Should I pray for that?

A few days later, I wrote in my journal:

I'm angry. Furious that I never get to run again. Every time I have to unsubscribe from a marathon email, or when a runner's gear ad shows up on my sidebar, I'm angry all over again. Yesterday while packing more boxes for the move, I came across my gels and fuel belts. I thought of the people I could give them to. People who don't have stupid broken hearts.

I'm reading about the Tabernacle right now. All this attention to detail – the golden pieces that have to be made in one piece, the thread woven together finely and precisely – all for God to come sit in the Holy of Holies, behind that curtain, and dwell in the midst of His people.

I can't help but think of my body — my stupid broken body. And how He loves it so much to come dwell in it.

And I think maybe I can make it another day without taking a quickened step. No matter how slow my pace, He is with me, in the body He designed with tender affection. The body that He loves. And that will be enough.

I struggled through the question of how to approach this new information about my heart. But when I thought about God, instead of about me, here's what I realized: He had revealed enough of His character to me through all the trials of the past year, through all the things I'd learned about Him in His Word, that I knew He was trustworthy, even when I didn't know the outcome. I could always assume the best of Him in every situation.

I decided to ask Him for healing. I decided that regardless of whether His answer was yes or no, it would be the kindest possible answer He could give. For the Prodigal Son, the famine that left him eating with the pigs was the best thing that could happen. It surely wasn't what he wanted, but it led him home. For Saul, the kindest thing was being struck blind and thrown from his horse. It ruined all his plans, but God revealed a far greater plan.

I resolved to trust that I'm not smart enough to know what's best for me, because even though I can't see the whole picture, I can trust the God who painted it. So I waited, I tried not to run, and I prayed:

Today, I choose to live under the poetry of Psalm 126, under the words of a foreign tongue whispered through unknown dimensions, landing in the thick air, settling on my heart. It presses into all the folds and creases of that quiet thudding muscle. It speaks the story of restoration, the promise of shouts of joy. I will not give up believing in You. You are the God who built my heart with Your own hands and planned all my days before You spoke the world. And You will keep me 'til You take me.

REFLECTION QUESTIONS:

1. Is it easy for you to assume the best of God's intentions? Why or why not? What aspects of His character inform the way you view Him?

2. Are there any things God is obligated to do? If so, what are they?

3. Do you trust God to keep you? Or do you feel like you have to fight for yourself and prove yourself?

37

FREEDOM

*For freedom Christ has set us free; stand firm therefore,
and do not submit again to a yoke of slavery.*
Galatians 5:1

I've exhausted myself for years, watching successes stack up against failures. I've felt the blows of vanity and insecurity, pride and despair, all stemming from the same root: my body. When I see the ads about how women always find themselves less attractive than they are, I can't relate. My problem is that I usually perceive myself as more attractive than I actually am.

When I look in the mirror, I see a stunning woman. This may sound like the perfect scenario, but it puts me at a disadvantage sometimes. For instance, when I see a photo or a video of myself, I think, "That is definitely not me, because I am clearly a knockout!"

A righteous relationship with food has always been just beyond my reach. While the bulk of my food choices are healthy ones, I'm bent toward gluttony, specifically toward mindless eating in social situations. I've always been jealous of the people who can get away with those little indiscretions, enjoying a handful of dark chocolate almonds at a Christmas party without wondering if their pants will fit on Monday. For me, there is no margin for error. Slight deviations from a strict diet have never paired well with my DNA.

For most of my life, I've been content to let vanity control my approach to gluttony (as though vanity were a lesser sin), instead of killing them both with equal vigilance. I exercised and ran my way through those occasional party cheats. But as Matt Chandler often says, pitting sin against sin is no path to freedom. My cardiologist's moratorium on running and weight-lifting effectively robbed me of that option anyway.

Instead, I prayed for obedience and discipline. I established the habit of yielding each food decision to God before I sat down to eat. "God, what's on the menu for this meal?" I asked. I stopped making promises to Him about how I was going to change, and I started asking Him to help me change. If He is my Lord and Master, if He owns the body He purchased on the cross, then He gets to call the shots, right? So I prayed and obeyed.

Vigilant obedience is a good thing, unless it is a means to an end instead of a means to God's glory. When I realized my "obedience" wasn't yielding the effect I'd hoped, I despaired. Surely my Lord and Master wanted me to be thin? Why weren't the pounds falling off in response to my yielding to Him? I began to monitor myself with greater detail.

This time, the sin in the ring with my gluttony had a pretty name that is listed among the Fruit of the Spirit: self-control. But this wasn't Spirit-prompted self-control; it was sinful control, fearful control. Since God and His menu weren't helping me, I needed to take back the reins. To paraphrase Stephen Charnock: "Not all cessation of sin is the mortification of it. A man may forsake one harlot and fall in love with another."

Calorie counting and attention to food origin were good things, but they had a way of taking up more brain space than the Gospel. They gradually consumed my thoughts. The mantra *"Results results results"* in the fitness freak is just another idolatrous version of the *"more more more"* we look down on in the glutton. That didn't sound like freedom to me – that sounded like bondage.

I'd pitted gluttony against everything I thought could take it down – vanity, vigilant obedience, sinful self-control – and I lost every time. Where was the freedom and victory His Word speaks of?

—

One morning when I was on tour, I sat alone at a restaurant staring at the handwritten menu. I had already gained three pounds during the month I'd been on tour. As I browsed the options, I asked Him my question. "God, what's on the menu for this meal?" But this time, instead of the "egg white omelette with spinach and tomato" I expected, I sensed a prompting in my spirit, a redirection. It felt like He asked me a question in reply: *What does a woman who is deeply loved by God eat for breakfast?*

I paused, thinking through the question:

"A woman who is deeply loved by God" doesn't gorge herself, trying to fill a void, because she finds satisfaction in the great love of God. "A woman who is deeply loved by God" doesn't starve herself, trying to win love and approval, because she rests in the great delight of her Father. That kind of woman doesn't measure herself against what she isn't, what she once was, or what she wants to be in the future, because she knows she is fully loved in the present.

Then I chose my meal. It was still the egg white omelette, but somehow my heart felt different – not fearful or punished, not like I was pulling myself up by my bootstraps or muscling through the act of obedience, hoping for a reward. Instead, my heart felt like it was being courted by a generous, loving, attentive King.

That has become the question I ask myself at every meal. As a result, I have different thoughts when I look in the mirror at the body my food choices had sustained, the choices made in response to God's great love: *"This is what the body of 'a woman who is deeply loved by God' looks like."* Even though that body looks mostly the same.

While scanning my journal recently, I found a theme in the way God had been speaking to me about all this. So much grace, so much encouragement from Him. I turned to a blank page and wrote out the things I sensed His Spirit saying to me:

- The thing I hate about the way He made me? It might be the very thing He uses to set others free. Satan accuses. God redeems.

- I can seek all I want, but I'll never get what He hasn't given (thoughts on 1 Samuel 23:14). He only gives what is best, so this is a good thing, not a threat.

- Attempting to claim His promises without Him reveals that my heart is after His blessing, not Him. It ends badly (thought on Numbers 14:39-45).

- Everything that passes through His hand and into my life is steeped in His kindness, intended for my fullness and joy (thoughts on Psalm 145:17).

- I will never be able to be good enough to earn the good gifts He has for me. He is the Giver. He gives His gifts in His time. And His gifts have never been based on my ability to achieve something for myself.

And these words, which felt like they were straight from Him:

- I just love you. I just do. Stop trying so hard.

~

Maybe my DNA isn't inferior after all. Maybe it's God's kindness toward me – His way of making sure I can't get away with favoring certain sins over others. Maybe my body and this struggle are two of the tools He is using to point me back to His great love and His total sufficiency.

God's love freed me up to eat to the glory of God. I was no longer wrapped up in weight gain or loss, no longer trying to sin my way out of a sin pattern. God loved me in my sin, and God loved me out of my sin. God loved me from bondage to freedom.

REFLECTION QUESTIONS:

1. What sin patterns do you feel stuck in? What have you tried to use as a means of escape? Did that press you further into sin or into freedom?

2. How would your life be different if every decision were made in light of your identity as "a person deeply loved by God"?

3. Whose approval are you trying to earn by behavioral modification? God's? Other people's? Your own?

4. Do you make promises to God about the ways you'll clean yourself up? Or do you ask God to help you and empower you with His Spirit? Why does the approach matter?

38

THE GOD WHO SEES

Your eyes saw my unformed substance;
in Your book were written, every one of them,
the days that were formed for me,
when as yet there was none of them.
How precious to me are Your thoughts, O God!
How vast is the sum of them!
Psalm 139:16-17

It's a fairly common struggle to wonder if God is really paying attention. Some people are certain He sees all their wrongs and will punish them. Others believe they can get away with anything, viewing God through the lens of their entitlement, as though He owes them blessing. It's difficult to hold a full, proper perspective on just how well God knows not only the desires of our hearts but the motives behind our actions.

—

I pulled my red Camry onto the front lawn of Butler Manor and popped the trunk. Raicheal and Meghann helped me carry my bags down the steps and stuff them into every available space. Raicheal loaded my cooler into the front floorboard, and Meghann brought six or seven beverages out to buckle into the passenger's seat.

"These should cover you until you get to Atlanta," she said, joking and patting the lid of a water bottle. Atlanta was only two hours away.

They hugged me and stepped onto the front porch, waving at me as I pulled off the lawn and onto Butler Avenue. Looking past the top of my silver hard-side suitcase and the neck of my guitar case in the backseat, I caught one last glimpse in the rearview mirror.

I thought about Butler Manor and D-Group and Greenville. I wasn't even sure if I wanted to leave Greenville or not. I still couldn't believe it existed – a town small enough that it didn't have the cost of living or traffic woes of a big city, but big enough that there were lush parks, modern restaurants, and all manner of culture, sports, the arts, and comedy. Blocks from my house, on Main Street, a picturesque waterfall cascaded beneath an elegant white and silver suspension bridge. It served as a popular meeting spot with D-Group girls.

Once, while having brunch at a restaurant by the river, overlooking the falls, my friend Dorothy said, "I feel like Greenville isn't a real city – it's a city in a movie." That summarized our town better than anything I'd ever heard.

I already missed it, even while I was driving away on its streets.

―

Two of my friends in Texas, a married couple, own a local organic market in Oak Cliff, one of the most hipster-hood areas of Dallas. That is to say, it has all the great new restaurants reviewed by *D Magazine*, but those restaurants are often located adjacent to liquor stores and vacant lots. Their market carries kombucha and grass-fed beef, and they have their own beehives on the roof and a coop of clucking chickens in the back.

One day, shortly after I moved to Dallas, we stood in their white-tiled kitchen talking and cooking dinner. Steven turned to me, chef's knife in hand, and said, "I got the results from that personality test I made you take."

Christine, who was five months pregnant, grabbed a sizzling square of sweet potato off the skillet and popped it into her mouth. "When he showed them to me, I was shocked at your results," she said. "But when I thought about it, I realized they make total sense." She wiped her tiny fingers on her apron and tucked a lock of her long black hair behind her ear.

The Culture Index Survey was the most detailed personality test I'd ever taken. It was pricey, too. I never would've paid to take it on my own; but after they had their employees at the market take it, one unused test remained, so they offered it to me for free.

"Why was it shocking?" I asked. I grabbed the container of cherry tomatoes from the stainless steel refrigerator and began slicing them on the bamboo cutting board.

"It ranked you as more autonomous than 99.75% of the population," Steven said.

"Crikey!" I said. "Then it's a good thing I'm living with the Chandlers right now. I hope I'm learning how to be less independent."

"Independence is not a bad thing, Tara-Leigh," Christine said, trying to encourage me. "God made you that way, and you're using it for His glory! You never would've launched out into ministry and speaking and singing and D-Groups if you didn't have that independent entrepreneurial streak."

"I trust there's truth in that and that He was intentional in building that into me. But I also think our greatest strengths are our greatest weaknesses. As far as the Kingdom is concerned, I want to be less *me, me, me* and more *us, you, Him*. You know? I've got a lot to learn, not just in case I want to be married someday, but even for ministry's sake."

The Chandlers' house was the perfect place to be learning. In fact, the lessons never even felt like lessons, never hit me with blunt force or rough edges. Instead, they came to me in such obvious ways, every day, like the way you can feel someone staring at you – intense, focused, weighted, but endearing (unless they're creepy).

My autonomy stared me down when I watched the way they loved each other, when I saw the way they served their neighbors, the way they raised their children. The first time I noticed how differently they lived occurred within 24 hours of moving in.

When I arrived after the 15 hour drive, LC had lit an amber scented candle, arranged lilies in a vase by my bed, and left the lamp on so I could see up the stairs. Matt gave me a tour of the house, showed me where the laundry room was, and told me where to park.

The next morning, I told LC, "I want to be good at this, so please tell me if I'm doing anything wrong. If I put a dish away in the wrong place, or if I'm too loud, or ... anything really. I receive correction well, and I'd rather have you tell me so I can learn and fix it."

"Everything is going to be great," she said, reassuring me with a smile as she wiped the marble countertop with a paper towel. "Oh, there is one thing! I noticed that you parked in the circle drive out front where Matt parks. Maybe instead of that, could you park down by the garage where I park?"

"Absolutely," I said. "Just so you know, I only parked there because that's where Matt said to park, but I can do whatever you guys want. I'm flexible."

"No, no," she said, "If Matt said that's where you should park, then that's good!"

Immediately, I noticed the way she respected him in her tone and her deference to what he had told me, but it took me another week before I fully understood what had transpired.

When the family flew out for a trip, they asked me if I could drive them to the airport. I dropped them off in their van, then returned to the house and parked the van in the garage. When I navigated the turns of the tight quarters, I realized: Matt told me to park near his car to keep me out of LC's way, and LC told me to park near her van to keep me out of Matt's way. They were deferring to each other.

I saw this kind of thing day after day. I took mental notes. I stood in awe of what it looked like to live as people who were not leaning into autonomy but into generosity, deference, and service. It seemed obvious it was one of the reasons God had seen fit to place me in their home. There was so much undoing that needed to happen in my heart – so much that still does.

One night, as they sat, snuggled up together on the brown leather couch in the living room, her hand on his knee, I looked at them from my spot on the matching loveseat.

"You know," I said, "I think you guys have ruined marriage for me."

"What are you talking about?" LC asked, laughing.

"My expectations are going to be too high. I have to keep reminding myself that you guys are 14 years deep in this. That you've learned and grown and fallen deeper in love."

They looked at each other and smiled. Matt made a googly face at her, crossing his eyes and giving a toothy grin, she laughed again and squeezed his knee.

"But seriously," I said, "if I ever get engaged, could I move out for about six months, and have him move in? Because I need him to see this."

I felt so known by God that He would place me in the middle of everything I needed to learn, while also making it a place I could find rest and guidance, and where I could invest.

How great His attention to the needs and desires of His children. He didn't just make us and leave us to find our own way – He is guiding us through the plan He has for us, for His glory, with love and tender affection. He surely is The God Who Sees.

REFLECTION QUESTIONS:

1. Do you feel like God sees you?

2. When do you feel forgotten by God?

3. What blessings in your life right now reveal that He's actually attentive to you, your needs, your desires?

4. If you really believed that God sees you, knows you, and attends to you, what effect would that have on your heart and mind? What would you gain?

39

REWARDER

*Whoever would draw near to God must believe that He exists
and that He rewards those who seek Him.*
Hebrews 11:6

There have been people who made me feel better. There have been people who made me want to be a better person. And then there have been people who actually made me become a better person. The kind who, when I'm spending time with them, seem to eradicate my weaknesses, fortify my strengths, purify me by the white hot flame of their own purity.

The first two feel more comforting and hopeful, but the last one feels more righteous and joy-inducing. When it comes to the people closest to me, I hope I will always choose the latter. That kind of love for Christ is contagious. That kind of love for Christ builds me up to love others well. If I have deep, healthy roots, my branches can reach further, provide more shade, bear more fruit to feed more people.

That's one of the reasons living with the Chandlers makes me feel more equipped in D-Group and writing and singing and worship leading. I have learned more simply from overhearing them talk than from many books or sermons I've consumed.

That isn't to say adjusting to my new life in Texas has been without struggle.

We live in the suburbs – which I don't love, because I'm a city girl at heart – where school zones are stacked on school zones. If you need to go anywhere at eight o'clock in the morning or three o'clock in the afternoon, it will take you five hours. (Not that I'm ever up at eight o'clock in the morning.) The upside of this is that, by contrast, the school-free summers make it feel like we live on the Autobahn.

Another thing I'm not used to is buying a tank of gas which is entirely depleted by sitting in all that school zone traffic. Steven and Christine, my friends who own the local organic market, bought a Vespa, and dropped their gas bill from $200 to $13 per month. Steven let me take it out for a spin one Sunday.

Five days later, I bought a cheap Vespa on Craigslist. (To be fair, it's not an actual Vespa, but when I told people I bought a scooter, they thought I meant one of the foot-propelled kinds that kids ride on playgrounds – a skateboard with a handle.) I named him Paolo. It's Italian for Paul.

You don't have to have a license to drive a Vespa if the engine is small enough, so people often accuse the drivers of having a revoked license because of a DUI. But maybe, like me, those tiny-engine Vespa owners don't want to spend a lot on gas. Or maybe, also like me, they just want to feel the wind in their hair and can't afford a convertible.

I ride my little scooter all over Highland Village. I drive alongside Ford F-450s, with four doors and six wheels. Farmers and construction workers hauling heavy loads cast shadows on me as we sit at red lights. They are always considerate. Texans. I may not love the suburbs, but I love these people.

I've always daydreamed about being the girl on the bike with a loaf of french bread and fresh flowers stuck in the wire basket on the front. Instead, I ended up being her more-European, carb-free cousin: kale and kombucha poking out of the little bag I hung behind Paolo's handlebars.

Despite becoming the woman of my daydreams, tooling around town on my scooter, I kept my Camry for longer trips and rainy days. One of the great things about the Camry is that I've basically turned it into my home on wheels. When I go on tour, I take 3 devices that make traveling 100% more awesome: a shiatsu massage chair that plugs into my cigarette lighter, an outlet/lighter adapter, and a travel blender. Once, while stuck in two hours of construction traffic in Mississippi, I got a massage and made myself a protein shake for dinner.

The Vespa had no bells and whistles though. It barely had enough room to hold my purse in a little storage space I referred to as "the trunk." Whenever I went to the store, I tucked my debit card and my license into my back pocket, leaving the trunk empty for my eggs and Greek yogurt.

One day I decided to ride the Vespa to Goodwill, in hopes that the lack of storage space would help me limit my purchases. I did not want to end up accidentally purchasing a bookshelf and a picnic basket when all I wanted was a jean jacket and a pair of closed-toe shoes.

The women's clothing section was in the back, so I walked past the aisles of plaid furniture and florist's vases and child safety seats stained with kool-aid. Overhead, "Billie Jean" came through the speakers. When "Billie Jean" comes on at Goodwill, watch out, because the entire store is about to break it down. Everyone was bopping their heads and mouthing the words. A woman reading the spines of romance novels on the left wall even started doing the two-hand finger snap while pumping her right knee back and forth.

I chuckled and shook my head. I walked to the beat of the music, afraid I'd be kicked out of the store if I dared to defy the unspoken agreement. It felt like one of those rare moments when everyone had unity of thought. I made eye contact with a man walking to the register and we nodded and smiled, as if to say to each other, *"Billie Jean was definitely not Michael Jackson's lover, and anyone who thinks otherwise is a fool!"*

There was a whole section of blue jean jackets, but none of them were styles I'd wear – either their backs and lapels were covered in sparkles and rhinestones, or they had roses embroidered on the shoulders. But at the far end of all the blue, there was one plain white jean jacket. I pulled it out to look at it. It was my size. Six dollars. *Sold!*

Walking past the shoe racks, I spotted a pair of dark green vintage loafers made of Italian leather. They were Salvatore Ferragamo. I laughed to myself, remembering the article I'd read about him at my cardiologist office. It kind of felt like God was giving me a head nod. They were my size. I picked up the shoes, knowing even at Goodwill they would cost more than I could afford, and flipped them over to see the price. *Twelve dollars!*

Delighted, I carried my white jacket and my green shoes to the register. The cashier checked out the woman ahead of me, piling stuffed animals and a board game into a plastic bag. Then he rang me up.

"Nine dollars," he said.

"No no, it should be eighteen," I told him, showing him the tag on the jacket and the chalked price on the soles of the shoes.

"Not today," he said, smiling. He pointed to a sign hanging from the ceiling. The sign had a phrase painted across the top that said, "Clothing items in these colors discounted 50%." Beneath it, there were two colored squares that appeared to be changed out daily. The squares for that day were green and white.

What?! It was such a little thing, but it made my eyes brim with tears. God's sweet kindness, showing up in a Goodwill to remind me how attentive He is.

~

The blessings kept coming. It felt like I couldn't turn around without someone giving me something for free – steak dinners, chiropractic visits, more steak, oil changes, and even more steak. Let's just say I ate well. Even after the grieving I'd done over the thought of no longer having a balcony where I could read my Bible in the morning, there was a balcony off my bedroom at the Chandlers' house.

I kept notes in my journal of all the ways He kept showing me kindness in Texas. Shortly after I got there, I wrote:

You are so generous. You've been so kind at every step. If You aren't calling me to stay here, You're doing a poor job of showing it. It feels like Your blessing is over every doorway I walk through.

I take care not to equate blessing with evidence that I'm being obedient. Scripture is filled with people who suffered because of their obedience. Namely, all the apostles and the early Church. But I also know we can't divorce His blessing from our lives either. In fact, He says we can't draw near to Him without believing He is a rewarder of those who seek Him. Those rewards may look different for each of us in different phases of life, and some of us may not see them until His return. But His heart toward us is a generous one. He can be trusted to give us the inheritance we have as His adopted children.

Everyone who has left houses or brothers or sisters or father or mother or children or lands, for My name's sake, will receive a hundredfold and will inherit eternal life. - Matthew 19:29

REFLECTION QUESTIONS:

1. When was a time you suffered for being obedient?

2. When was a time your obedience prevented suffering?

3. What stories from Scripture display those different results of obedience?

4. If it's possible that obedience can result in suffering, then what

does it mean that God is a "rewarder of those who seek Him"?

40

REWARD

After these things the word of The Lord came to Abram in a vision, saying, "Do not be afraid, Abram. I am your shield, your exceedingly great reward."
Genesis 15:1 (NKJV)

I'm about to say something that may sound shocking or arrogant: it does not surprise me that God loves me.

That's not what I'm supposed to say, right? Because I'm a terrible sinner, and He's perfect, so I should be totally unloveable. And I am. But for His glory and through Christ's death, the Father adopted me into His family, to be His heir and carry out His heritage. It logically follows that a God who would go to such great lengths to have a relationship with me would love me in and through and because of and for that relationship.

What does not make sense to me *at all* is that I love Him.

He's infinitely lovable, more beautiful than all other desires ... but

I was born with a wicked heart, one that is bent in toward myself, one that takes tiny created things and makes them into gods that I could easily spend my life worshipping. I'm inherently unable to view things through a lens of truth. Truth is all around me, to be sure, but my natural eyes are too dim to see it.

It continues to shock me to find myself growing more in love with Him all the time – when I want to read His Word, or when I want to obey Him more than I want to do my own thing. I know that it must be His love for me working within me to produce this love for Him, because I don't know how to love good things on my own.

We love because He first loved us. - 1 John 4:19

I'm stunned by my love for Him, because it is the most gripping, obvious, undeniable evidence of His love for me. Scripture says that the only reason we love Him is because He loved us first. I used to read 1 John 4:19 as though it only indicated the order in which our love happened, but what it really means is that His love is the cause of our love. Our love is the very fruit of His love.

He initiates, sustains, and fulfills all the things involved in that love relationship.

What a glorious victory is ours.
Mostly we sat on the bench.
We never carried the ball into the end zone.
Some days we took the field and ran until our legs burned,
But you never pressed your shoulder into the opponent,
And I never caught the game winning touchdown.
Still, we roar like champions,
Decked in rings and baptized in celebration,
We hail the one who won it all.
We share in His glory,
We dance in His ticker tape parade.
What a glorious victory is His,
And ours,

Because He shares.

The poet Kahlil Gibran got many things wrong, but he said one thing that resonates with me: "The deeper sorrow carves into your being, the more joy you can contain." The joy of The Lord has been sticking to me lately, leaving its fragrance on my skin. Just by breathing, I am reminded.

Over the course of a year, His kindness showed up in so many places:

- I was diagnosed with an often fatal medical condition while in a 2nd world country and denied the freedom to come back to the States, until God healed me instantly.

- My dad had an injury moments before I arrived to see him. God timed things in such a way to put me in the path of a stranger who revealed that it was a heart attack, then dad led his nurse to Christ and came home safely.

- My sister was given a death sentence, and we watched her dying in a pronounced, dramatic way. Then God shocked even her world-renowned brain surgeon by reversing her cancer. (And now she leads a D-Group!)

Lately, I feel the love of the Father in such obvious ways that I'm carrying it through all my moments. "It will subside in time," the cynic would say. All the more reason to speak it boldly now, because I know it is the forever truth.

As I lean more into His love, I find more reasons to delight in Him. I can hardly keep myself from talking about His great love for us. He is so sweet to let hardships draw us to Himself.

All these life circumstances are the waves throwing me against the Rock of Ages. The ocean of life is always undulating, the tides always moving with the moon and gravity, all the other things rising and falling at His orchestration.

God is our refuge and strength,
a very present help in trouble.
Therefore we will not fear though the earth gives way,
though the mountains be moved into the heart of the sea,
though its waters roar and foam,
though the mountains tremble at its swelling.
- Psalm 46:1-3

As I wait to see if He will heal my heart, as I wait to see what will happen in my singleness, I'm learning that it's okay to want things that haven't happened. Contentment and longing aren't mutually exclusive. It's okay to feel those desires – He can be trusted to do what is best with them.

Sometimes, He does even better things than I imagine, because His ability to bless exceeds my capacity to hope. But it's best for my heart to sing His praises in the meantime, from the crest of every wave, not just when I see how it ends.

—

Dear The Lord,

Every day feels like it surely must be the first day I've ever really loved You – all clumsy and excited and hopeful and filled with longing. You never bore me, You never grow old. You are endlessly fascinating and beautiful and kind. Every wound I've encountered at the waves of Your hand has evoked a deeper, truer praise from my lips, because You keep revealing more of who You are with the rolling of the tides.

Someday maybe we will walk on water. But until then, as I wait for the redemption of all things, keep the whole of me anchored in You, so no matter the storm, I will never be moved. You are my exceedingly great Reward.

The Lord is my chosen portion and my cup;
You hold my lot.
The lines have fallen for me in pleasant places;
indeed, I have a beautiful inheritance.

- Psalm 16:5-6

REFLECTION QUESTIONS:

1. What aspects of God's character are most delightful to you? What characteristics are the hardest to grasp or appreciate?

2. What keeps you from valuing God above all other things?

3. How can actively delighting in God's character change the way you live?

ABOUT TLC

Tara-Leigh Cobble is the author of five books and is a frequent speaker at events for women, singles, college, and youth. She also leads worship and performs concerts around the world. She loves puffins, but has never met one in real life (bucket list!) and she's terrified of octopuses.

In 2009, she launched D-Group (Discipleship Group) Ministries with nine strangers in a living room. Today, she leads hundreds of women in living rooms around the world as part of weekly D-Group meetings. You can find out more information about D-Group – what it is, and how to join or start one – here: www.mydgroup.org

Tara-Leigh lives in suburban Dallas. She has no pets, plants, or children, or anything else that might die if she forgets to feed it. Despite that, she lives with two adults, three children, a dog, and several plants, all of which are still alive (except – full disclosure – the succulent).

WWW.TARALEIGHCOBBLE.COM
WWW.MYDGROUP.ORG